Shift into a Higher Gear

Other Books by Delatorro McNeal, II

Shift Into a Higher Gear: Better Your Best and Live Life to the Fullest Companion Workbook

Platinum Presentations: 52 Tips to Speak with Confidence, Win Your Audience and Grow Your Bank Account

Thriving Through Your Storms: 12 Profound Lessons to Help you Grow Through Anything you Go Through in Life

Caught Between a Dream and a Job: How to Leave the 9 to 5 Behind and Step Into the Life You've Always Wanted

Shift into a Higher Gear

Better Your Best and Live Life to the Fullest

DELATORRO McNEAL, II

BK
Berrett–Koehler Publishers, Inc.

Berrett-Koehler Publishers, Inc.   Tel: (510) 817-2277
1333 Broadway, Suite 1000   Fax: (510) 817-2278
Oakland, CA 94612-1921   www.bkconnection.com

ORDERING INFORMATION

Quantity sales. Special discounts are available on quantity purchases by corporations, associations, and others. For details, contact the "Special Sales Department" at the Berrett-Koehler address above.

Individual sales. Berrett-Koehler publications are available through most bookstores. They can also be ordered directly from Berrett-Koehler: Tel: (800) 929-2929; Fax: (802) 864-7626; www.bkconnection.com.

Orders for college textbook / course adoption use. Please contact Berrett-Koehler: Tel: (800) 929-2929; Fax: (802) 864-7626.

Distributed to the U.S. trade and internationally by Penguin Random House Publisher Services.

Berrett-Koehler and the BK logo are registered trademarks of Berrett-Koehler Publishers, Inc.

Printed in Canada

Berrett-Koehler books are printed on long-lasting acid-free paper. When it is available, we choose paper that has been manufactured by environmentally responsible processes. These may include using trees grown in sustainable forests, incorporating recycled paper, minimizing chlorine in bleaching, or recycling the energy produced at the paper mill.

Library of Congress Cataloging-in-Publication Data

Names: McNeal, Delatorro L., author.
Title: Shift into a higher gear : better your best and live life to the
    fullest / Delatorro McNeal, II.
Description: First Edition. | Oakland, CA : Berrett-Koehler Publishers,
    2021. | Includes bibliographical references and index. | Summary: "This
    book shows us how to move beyond cursory, fearsome living by kicking
    full-throttle into a life that is vast and deep"— Provided by
    publisher.
Identifiers: LCCN 2021026207 (print) | LCCN 2021026208 (ebook) | ISBN
    9781523093731 (paperback) | ISBN 9781523093748 (adobe pdf) | ISBN
    9781523093755 (epub)
Subjects: LCSH: Self-actualization (Psychology) | Motivation (Psychology)
Classification: LCC BF637.S4 M3956 2021 (print) | LCC BF637.S4 (ebook) |
    DDC 158.1--dc23
LC record available at https://lccn.loc.gov/2021026207
LC ebook record available at https://lccn.loc.gov/2021026208

First Edition

27 26 25 24 23 22   10 9 8 7 6 5 4 3 2

Cover designer: Wes Youssi, M80 design. Author photo: @NeilLeePhoto.
Illustrations: Silke Bachmann. Book producer and text designer: Leigh McLellan Design.
Copyeditor: Michele Jones. Proofreader: Mary Hazlewood. Indexer: Ken Dellapenta.

*I dedicate this book to you and the next
level that you are seeking through this book.
I am confident that if you take action on what
you learn, you will manifest your goals, dreams,
and aspirations and fulfill the title of this book.*

Namaste. Amen. And So It Is

Contents

Foreword

Allow me to personally congratulate you on the transformational journey that you're about to go on with Delatorro McNeal, II, your guide in this powerful book *Shift into a Higher Gear*. I've enjoyed a forty-plus-year career in the personal and professional development industry, and about ten years ago, I met Delatorro at a National Speakers Association convention, where he was earning the coveted CSP designation. When I met him, I knew he was a young man marked for greatness. Over the years, we've shared the stage at several events, including some of my own, and I've admired his dynamic, high-energy, high-content presentations. I've seen the powerful impact that Delatorro's content has on audiences. And now you will get the opportunity to learn from Delatorro's wisdom in this exciting and edgy book.

I am a huge fan and advocate of lifelong learning and constant growth and improvement. It's a hallmark of all high achievers. In fact, I've been fortunate enough to travel to 125 countries and speak to over five million people all over the world, and one thing I know for sure is that people everywhere want the content Delatorro shares in this book. Everyone wants to shift into their next level. We all want to top our last best performance, and we all want to live life to the fullest. Ambition is a trait of any success-ful person, and I love that *Shift into a Higher Gear* challenges you to aspire higher and to take your best and top it!

I believe that regardless of your professional title or career field, personal development and growth are at the center of all professional success. In fact, I always teach that you can never outperform your own self-concept. *Shift into a Higher Gear* will challenge you to develop in many areas that will then ripple out and impact your professional life in ways that you can't even imagine. The truth is that we all want to matter, we all want to count, and we all want to leave this world better than the way we found it—and this book will help you do so.

I enthusiastically applaud Delatorro for creating something new and fresh in the personal development space. This is the first time that I've seen such a powerful parallel drawn between motorcycle riding and personal development. Delatorro has masterfully built a memorable and profound message around how riding a motorcycle can be a metaphor for life and business success. Whether you've ever ridden a motorcycle or not, you will enjoy this book and profit from it.

Delatorro is an expert in instructional design, and his commitment to helping you get the most out of this book is evident by the practical elements he has built into it. From the various learning exercises throughout the book to the reflection moments, profound questions he asks you, and journaling assignments, he skillfully connects the basic fundamentals of motorcycle riding to keys that we need in order to shift our own lives to that elusive next level that we all desire. There is so much meat in this book, and I love that from beginning to end the focus is entirely on you as the reader. It's aimed directly at helping you shift—now!

I personally resonate with this book especially because in my twenties and thirties I owned a motorcycle myself. Two, in fact. I traveled the country taking many trips with friends and by myself. I've slept next to my bike at night and performed maintenance on my bike as needed. I can attest firsthand to the exhilarating feelings of being a motorcycle rider, and I can also attest to the exhilarating feelings of becoming one of the best in my industry and developing myself to the fullest. There are indeed many parallels, and I know that you'll enjoy how Delatorro draws on these congruencies while showing you in a very tactical, practical, and methodical way exactly how you can learn and apply these principles to get maximum results.

If you're ready to accelerate your success and roll the throttle of your goals and dreams, then it's time for you to shift into a higher gear with Delatorro. I can't think of a better time than right now for you to better your best and live life to the fullest.

Brian Tracy
Best-selling author of *Eat That Frog!*, *Goals!*, and many other books

Your Invitation to the Ride of Your Life

Congratulations! You've just begun what I am sure will be a magnificent adventure, and I am honored and excited to be your guide along this powerful and transformational journey. Let me say from the outset that it doesn't matter if you've never ridden a motorcycle, have zero or even little interest in riding a motorcycle, rode in the past, or ride presently; the goal and purpose of this book is to teach you and, in some cases, simply remind you of powerful life lessons that I've gleaned while incorporating motorcycle riding into my life as a hobby for the last ten-plus years. You don't have to be a biking enthusiast or a current rider, but let me warn you: by the time you're done learning about the various parallels that exist between your life and motorcycle riding, you just may want to welcome this amazing mode of transportation and transformation into your life.

A Motorcycle Is a Metaphor

This book is an invitation for you to become your best self and to level up multiple times. It's also an opportunity for you to enroll in the next level of your life, on your terms. You're about to gain some amazingly profound knowledge about how various aspects of motorcycle riding mirror and model your life, career, and/or business. Let me warn you—once you've finished reading this book and, more important, started to apply the principles within, you're never going to see a motorcycle the same way again.

Because from now on, when you see a motorcycle, you will see your life. You're going to be able to dissect the various aspects of a motorcycle, and doing so will immediately cause you to take an introspective look into your life and/or career and determine what you need to do next in order to shift into a higher gear.

What if I told you everything about motorcycle riding parallels some aspect of your life? From the brakes to the wheels, to the engine, to how to ride, to how you balance the bike, to how you roll the throttle, and even whom you ride with. What if all of it mirrored your life and career in some way? Wouldn't that be cool? Well, buckle up, because that's exactly the adventure you're about to take. Sound good?

For many people, a motorcycle is simply a metaphor for something in life that they're needlessly afraid of. Think about something right now that you want to grow, develop, or take to that next level, but you're not doing it because you're afraid. This book will show you exactly how to step into that thing with full confidence. People often say that motorcycles are dangerous, and I agree, but so are cars, planes, scooters, roller coasters, cruise ships, helicopters, and simply crossing the street these days. It's all dangerous. However, just because something is dangerous doesn't mean you shouldn't do it. You take calculated blind-trust risks every single day. Ride with caution; but please, let's ride!

● ● ●

Imagine that you're riding in your car on a beautiful sunny day and you come up to a red light. As you wait, a really nice motorcycle pulls up right next to you—and for a split second, you become enthralled imagining the experience that you know the rider is having. You wonder where they're going and where they may be coming from. And, for that split second, you kind of want to be them. The bike looks and sounds so cool; it's clean, it's stylish, and the people on it look as though they are having the best time of their lives. For a moment, you kind of wish you could trade in your car and be on that motorcycle.

Has that ever happened to you? Well, that happened to me for years! I would be riding in my car, minding my own business; a really cool motorcycle would pull up beside me, and I would immediately go into this trance, because I knew that in that moment, there was a level of life that I wasn't living. There were experiences that I wasn't having. There were opportunities that I wasn't taking full advantage of because I had not yet shifted into a higher gear.

So I'm curious: What thoughts and feelings come up for you when you see a motorcycle? Please write them down here.

_____

_____

_____

_____

This is your first interactive opportunity in this book. As we go along through this book, you'll see various places where I ask you to interact with me. Please participate fully, because you'll get the most out of this book by doing so.

Have you ever ridden a motorcycle before? Have you ever experienced the sheer thrill of the wind blowing in your face? Ever felt the vibration of the engine roaring underneath you like a lion? Have you ever felt the rush of adrenaline flow through your body as you race from 0 to 70 mph or faster in only a few seconds, with the wind hitting your body powerfully?

It's quite a rush. And I firmly believe that life is supposed to be a rush as well. Not 100% of the time, of course, but it's supposed to be an adventure, a dance . . . a motorcycle ride! Think about it: we've all heard the expression, "live life to the fullest," right? Well, when you hear that, what does that mean to you?

Are you currently living your life to the fullest, according to your own definition?

Yes or no?

The tragedy of life is not that it ends so soon, but that we wait so long to begin it. —W. M. Lewis

My Bike Experience

I've been riding a motorcycle for roughly ten years. I'm pleased and blessed to report that in more than ten years of owning my motorcycle, I've never once had an accident. However, during those ten years, riding that same motorcycle has taught me some of the most profound lessons about life and business that I've ever learned. That's right—some of the greatest principles that I've learned about life and business haven't come from seminars, haven't come from other books, and haven't come from mentors, even though all of these outlets have taught me so much amazing stuff that I love, value, and appreciate.

After riding my motorcycle for about two years, I began to start receiving what I call divine downloads about how things I was experiencing on my bike rides parallel important lessons for life and business. Each time I would take my motorcycle out, I would get a different message, illustration, metaphor, or life principle. I began to journal about these insights and save them. About a year later, I was invited to speak at a large event, so I asked whether I could make my presentation an illustrated speech by bringing my motorcycle on stage. It was a huge hit. I then gave that same presentation, back then called "Living Life Full Throttle," several more times—each time live with my motorcycle on stage. After the fifth time giving that presentation, I knew that I was on to something unique and extremely powerful because I had never seen a speaker use a motorcycle as a prop and teach such profound metaphors using it as I was. In 2013, I turned that illustrated keynote speech into a four-day conference called the Full Throttle Experience. Using experiential learning techniques, I taught high-achieving career professionals and entrepreneurs how to get the most out of their lives, push passed their limitations, heal from the disappointments of life, and roll the throttle by taking massive action on their dreams. Until now, the principles you're about to read in this book were taught only at my conference. And I am blessed to now be able to expand the reach of this content through my partnership with Berrett-Koehler Publishers and share the lessons that I've seen transform the lives of so many through my live events, and help you shift into a higher gear so that you can better your best and live life to the fullest.

Why This Book Now?

I firmly believe that when the student is ready, the teacher appears. Something about where you are in your life right now has attracted this book to you as a very powerful solution. You may not even know this, but you're ready for something different. You are ready for a shift of some sort in your life. Otherwise, you wouldn't pick up a book with this title. I am honored to serve as a teacher in your life through this literary experience.

In 2016, the global health care brand Abbott conducted a study, surveying two million people globally.[1] The survey asked participants to identify the key indicators of a fulfilling life.

- 32% said family
- 12% said success
- 8% said giving
- 7% said health

Of these four, which would you rate as the most important indicator of your living a fulfilling life?

When the survey participants were asked to name the top barriers to living a fulfilling life, here were their responses:

- 44% said money
- 33% said time
- 20% said work
- 18% said priorities

Would you say that these are the same barriers you face when it comes to living the quality of life that you desire? Well, this book addresses what's holding you back and exactly how you can move forward powerfully.

The study also found that on a 1–100 scale, the global average for people rating themselves as fulfilled in their lives was 68, meaning that globally, we are failing at living a fulfilling life. Here are the ten countries with the highest average fulfillment ratings:

1. China
2. Costa Rica

3. Columbia

4. Mexico

5. Indonesia

6. Thailand

7. Peru

8. Germany

9. Philippines

10. Malaysia

The United States ranked 65th on the scale, which is just below the global average.

Take a moment and journal about what this research means to you personally and how it can help to shape and frame how you want to shift into a higher gear so that you can better your best and live life to the fullest.

Shift into a Higher Gear is a crucial read at this point in human history because I believe that globally—as the research I've just cited indicates, humanity is asking very similar questions. In my travels as a top-ranked peak performance expert and global keynote speaker, I've experienced unique "laboratories" for the last twenty years. Having worked with top organizations and spoken for very prestigious conventions, I've learned that we human beings are very similar in our desires for that ever-elusive "next level." Everyone wants to top himself or herself, and I've never met a single person who doesn't want to be the best in their industry or at their profession and craft. We all want to lead fulfilling lives and mean something. I also have learned that we all need that push, jolt, and springboard that will propel us into that next place. I firmly believe that this book is it for you. Let's be honest: the global pandemic of 2020 caused humanity a moment of pause. It made all of us rethink what we want most in life.

In my keynote speeches that I deliver globally to audiences both live and virtually, I often teach about change. And one of the ideas that I always share is that change takes place at two speeds: revolutionary and evolutionary—in other words, fast change and slow change. But what's interesting is that when I ask most audiences and most people whether they'd like change to be slow or fast, they always want fast change. On a motorcycle, if you want to manifest what you want faster, then you've got to shift into a higher gear. Most people want what they want—just faster. Whether it's paying off debt, obtaining their dream home, being forgiven for a mistake they made, finding their ideal soul mate, losing weight, reuniting family members, getting in better shape, building their wealth portfolio, traveling for fun, or just learning new skills—most people want what they want . . . just faster. So to get it faster, you're going to have to shift into a higher gear! in this book, I'll show you how to get that faster.

How to Get the Most out of This Book

Research suggests that to get the most out of any learning experience, the learner/reader must be in an active learning state. This goes against the traditional way that we were taught. Most of us were taught in very passive learning environments. This book, by contrast, is designed to make you participate in the learning. It's been proven that retention of content explodes to 70%–90% when a person is in active learning mode when they're learning the material. I mention all of this because my goal is for you to have a learning experience with this book. It's literally a seminar on paper. I don't want you to read it passively. I want you to read it actively. So I've intentionally built in many exercises and activities, and I've even put in spaces where I want you to actually write in this book. Your feedback as we go through this process will be invaluable and essential to your overall success. My master's degree is in instructional systems design and performance enhancement, and I've written this book in such a way that you will be able to get the most out of it.

If I were you, I'd get a special journal just for this book and the many revelations and lessons that it will unpack for you. I encourage you to write in it, answer questions in it, and process your thoughts and feelings and the actions steps that you'll be inspired to take as a result of what you encounter. In addition, I am a big believer that success is better together. I strongly suggest that you find someone to experience this book with. They can be a friend, colleague, coworker, significant other, family member, business associate, or just someone who has similar goals, ambition, drive, and standards of excellence that you do.

Each chapter title starts with an action verb intentionally. Each chapter also concludes with a list titled "Five Ways You Can Shift Higher and Tune Up the Motorcycle of Your Life." These are reminders to help you keep up with the maintenance of your bike so that you can achieve the optimal use of it. They are also meant to remind you of the content that's most powerful to help you prepare for the next chapter. The goal is to make you take massive action or, as I like to say, *"Roll the Throttle."* Because the throttle of your life is always taking intelligent and consistent action toward your desires. That's what the throttle represents: you hitting the gas pedal in life, business, and career so you can get moving in the direction you really want to go. You'll learn more about that later in the book. With five action steps per chapter, you'll be exposed to more than sixty different action steps you can take to help you arrive at your destination and enjoy the ride at the same time.

In addition, at the end of the book there's a thirty-plus-question Discussion Guide designed to make you think about all the various ways you can apply what you've learned to your life; that's what I want for you. We've also built a website with a variety of bonus content that just didn't make it into this book. Make sure you visit www.ShiftIntoAHigherGear.com and enroll for free in our global online Shift Higher Biker Community. You'll want to join our Facebook page as well. Our goal is to rally readers of this book from all over the globe so that we can support, encourage, and inspire one another to do exactly what the title of this book suggests!

P.S. One final thing. Remember that you will always find whatever you're looking for. Look for big and small breakthroughs as you read. Open yourself up to the possibility that you will experience breakthroughs throughout this book, and that's exactly what will happen for you, because they are everywhere. OK . . . are you ready? Let's grow!

CHAPTER 1

Shift Small Things to Make a Big Difference

—————————————

Off the top of your head, when you hear the phrase *shift into a higher gear*, what comes to mind?

_____

_____

_____

_____

_____

_____

I ask this question because inherent in the title of this book is a very powerful and life-altering command. It came, without your permission, and has already gone directly into your subconscious mind! Yep, that's right—I'm using my Jedi mind tricks on you already. But seriously, I want you to think about what's already bubbling up for you when you process the title. Go ahead—reread it if you need to. *Shift . . . into a higher gear.*

By the time you're done with this book, that phrase will mean something much more powerful than it does at this moment. I want us to have a starting point for what this phrase exemplifies in your life now. Understand that its definition will shift as we go through this book.

Small, Steady Changes

By definition, *shift* means "to move or cause to move from one place to another, especially over a small distance." Think about that for a second. Shifts don't have to be these huge, massive, super-grand gestures of change. Sometimes it can be small things that make a big difference. My goal is to get you to make small tweaks in what you're already doing that will make a monumental difference in your immediate and long-term results. Another definition of *shift* is "a slight change in position, direction, or tendency." See . . . there it goes again. The notion that big changes can only happen in big shifts is completely inaccurate! Small ones (i.e., slight changes or small distances) can and will actually get the job done just as nicely, if not better.

We've been lied to for most of our lives. We were all told that we had to make astronomical, enormous, and opulent changes in order to get the results we desire. For many of us, we have been left feeling like under-achievers— unsuccessful, unmotivated, or simply flat-out "not committed enough" to get the outcomes we want. I can use myself as an example.

For years, I struggled with managing my weight. I would constantly fluctuate between 210 and 250 pounds. I blamed it on the fact that I traveled too much to be consistent with a complex exercise and nutrition plan. But the moment I stopped making excuses and started making small changes in my nutrition and my exercise, I was able to get to my ideal size and feel great about my body. I had to recognize that small changes were just as potent as huge ones.

I believe that we focus too much on making massive changes instead of small, steady ones. This causes us to give up way too soon and settle for mediocrity, usually because of habits and thought processes. But greatness and excellence are at the finish line if we don't forfeit them.

Here are some things you see daily, but whose hidden meanings you overlook:

- Big trucks rolling on small tires
- Big doors swinging on small hinges
- Big boats gliding effortlessly because of small propellers
- Big building architectural designs drawn on small plans

- Big companies merging in small boardrooms
- Big ideas written out on small napkins, over a business lunch
- Big adults starting off as small embryos
- Big forests beginning with small seeds in the ground
- Big movements being initiated by small, yet powerful, groups of individuals
- Big amounts of wealth being controlled by a small percentage of the population

The point is that it's the small things that make the biggest differences in your life and business. And it's going to be the small things that make the most powerful difference for you as well. This reminds me of the *Pareto principle*, otherwise known as the 80/20 Rule.

20% of your effort produces 80% of your results.

20% of your wardrobe produces 80% of your outfits.

20% of employees produce 80% of the results in most companies.

20% of donors create 80% of the revenue for most nonprofits.

Get it?

Only 20% of what you do daily is producing 80% of your actual results. The other 80% is what we call superfluous! It's filler, not exactly necessary to the bottom line. The key to success, then, becomes finding out what your magic 20% is, and doing *that* 80% of the time. That's how you 10× your results in life and business. That's how you shift into a higher gear. We're going to talk about a lot of this, and so much more. But again, it all goes back to the power of making shifts.

For example, we all know that 211° water is extremely hot; however, it doesn't produce steam until it's heated one extra degree. At exactly 212°, something magical happens. That superhot water transforms into steam, and steam powers locomotives, trains, ships, and all types of amazing machinery. What's my point? What if I told you that you are only one shift away from a transformational moment in your life, career, money, relationships, parenting, physical health, business, ministry, and/or emotions? Most times, we feel as though we are miles and light-years away from the things we want. What I've learned is that most people are simply a few shifts away from breakthrough. That's exactly what I will prove to you in this book.

When I became a dad, I made a small shift in my parenting style. I made a decision not just to parent my girls but also to mentor and coach them to greatness. I made it my goal not just to provide for their needs but to be intentional about their goals and aspirations. I purposely invest in them, teach them lessons that my mentors taught me, and coach them through the mountaintops and valley-lows of their lives. That one small shift took me from 211° to 212° of steam-powered, locomotive, ninja-dad status that I am grateful for every single day.

Please allow me now to give you a few questions to ponder based on what I've already shared with you. Feel free to journal about your answers to these simple yet powerful questions.

- What small people shifts do you need to make right now?
- What small nutritional shifts do you need to make right now?
- What small financial shifts do you need to make right now?
- What small personal growth shifts do you need to make right now?
- What small emotional shifts do you need to make right now?
- What small parenting shifts do you need to make right now?
- What small spiritual shifts do you need to make right now?

I invite you to answer these questions, and I invite you to take some small action today to make a few of the changes you thought about as you answered them. Remember, this entire book is an invitation for you to shift higher in any and every area of your life that you want to. Keep in mind, this book is not called *Think about Shifting into a Higher Gear*. It is titled very intentionally, because I want you to take the action and actually shift. Deal? OK cool!

A Higher Gear

Congratulations! A "higher gear" denotes that you are already doing something right—which you are! You are already a rock star. Only a rock star would be drawn to a book like this. I firmly believe that like attracts like. I firmly believe that you and I were drawn to this cocreated learning experience because you're already on the journey to success and you just want to shift some things into a higher gear. Well, guess what? I do too! Let's do this thing together, then—shall we?

We are about to go from good to great and from OK to amazing! It doesn't matter where you are currently; we are about to level up. It's all going into a higher gear.

I need you to understand something: I'm proud of you. Take a minute and really embrace those words. Most high achievers do not hear this phrase nearly enough. Although I personally heard it as a kid, I did not hear it enough. And I think that's why today, as an adult, I am such a celebrator, encourager, and exhorter of humanity. I believe that deep down, all of us want someone to be genuinely, sincerely, and enthusiastically proud of us.

- Proud of our efforts and progress
- Proud of our journey and resilience
- Proud of our hustle and determination
- Proud of our results

We all want that! So again, I am very proud of you. And I am excited about your current level and your next level. A popular inspirational says, "Failure is not an option. It's actually a privilege, reserved exclusively for those who try." That's why I can say that I'm proud of you—for trying! It's in the effort that success is truly discovered. But now that we have covered that, I need you to understand something else even more powerful.

There is No "There" *There!*

It's important that you understand that there is no "there" *there.* Allow me to explain. If your entire motivation in life is to get to a place called *there,* the challenge with getting *there* is finding out the truth about what doesn't exist there. So you have to ask yourself what really drives you once you get *there.*

As I said earlier, since 2013, I've hosted a powerful annual conference for high achievers called the Full Throttle Experience. It's a personal development conference where I teach and instill many principles you will learn in this book, through a high-energy motivational and experiential immersion process that creates lasting change for attendees all over the world. That event (my *there*) takes about six months for my staff and me to plan and market, and four days to execute. But in total honesty, the final day of the event is the least fulfilling day for me personally. That's right. When it's all over, it's the hardest day for me, because while yes, I am a million percent grateful for all the changes and transformations that people make during the four days, saying good-bye to everyone and tearing down all the banners, lights, and activity stations is kind of sad for me. Why? Because there is no there *there*. The truth is, the best part of the conference is the process of the conference and the execution of the conference, not its completion.

Have you ever achieved a goal, and once you have, you still weren't happy with what you got? Why is it that we can put all this effort into achieving a goal, get it, and ultimately still not be happy with what we got? I believe that success in life is ultimately not about just arriving as much as it is about the journey. Which means we cannot be motivated by the *there*; we must be motivated by the process of getting there. Which means we must be excited about enjoying the ride. And every single day, with each sunrise you are fortunate to experience, life gives you a chance to enjoy the ride.

I believe that in order to enjoy the ride, you must "better" your best. Part of the disease of being a high achiever is that we always want to improve, we always want to get better, and we always want to top ourselves. Every time we are about to score a touchdown, we push the end zone back about twenty-five yards! If you're reading this book, that means you're a high achiever and probably an admitted overachiever. You're in good company, because so am I. I don't know any high achievers who are not competitive, who are not movers and shakers, who are not go-getters, and who are not people who want the best out of life. But for us to enjoy the journey, must we not only attain the best but on a regular basis outdo our best, because that's how we feel fulfilled.

Life's Daily Invitation

I remember back in October of 2016, the first time I spoke for the Million Dollar Round Table. It was my largest speaking engagement to date. I was speaking to over ten thousand of the top financial professionals from eighty-three countries all around the world. As I was speaking, my presentation was being translated into thirteen different languages simultaneously. It was amazing. A seminal moment in my career. It went so well, I got invited back the following year. I clearly remember beginning my thirty-nine-minute keynote address with the following thesis.

I believe that life gives us one open invitation daily. It comes in the form of a question: Will you be better today than you were yesterday? Asking yourself this causes you to make a constant decision to better your best. I believe it's easy for us to better our best because our best is really and truly based on our past. Here are some questions that will help you see where I'm going with this:

- Where was the best vacation you've ever taken?
- What's the best month in sales you've ever had?
- When was the best spur-of-the-moment trip you took?
- What's the best sporting event you've ever attended?
- How was the best steak restaurant you've enjoyed?
- What's the best family dinner you've ever prepared?
- What's the best play you've ever seen?
- Remember the best concert you've ever attended?
- What's the best book you've ever read (besides this one, of course)?

Any questions asked about your best will automatically make your brain reference one place and one place only. That place is in your past. Your best is always based on yesterday, yester-week, yester-month, yester-year, and sometimes even yester-decade. Our best is always predicated on experiences we've already had, period. That's why it's so easy to better our best: our best is based on something that has already happened, which means we must use today to improve our tomorrow.

Every single day, we get a chance to top ourselves. To better ourselves! And that's what "the best" do: they consistently improve themselves and better their last execution of success. The Japanese call this *kaizen*. Global peak performance expert Tony Robbins in 1980 coined the term *CANI*, which stands for Continuous and Never-ending Improvement.

The late, great Godfather of Soul, James Brown, was asked in an interview, "Mr. Brown, out of all your concerts and performances that you've done all over the world, which one was your best?" Brown quickly responded, "The one I'm going to do tomorrow night!" James Brown was the best because he made a commitment to constantly shift his performances into a higher gear and top himself night after night. What about you?

The biggest room in the world is always, room for improvement! —Author unknown

The 1% Shift

So the first minor shift that I want you to adopt that will make a major difference in your entire life is the 1% shift. I want you to commit to getting 1% better every single day in one area of your life and business/career that you care about. That's right. Notice I didn't ask you to get 10% better, 45% better, or 80% better. All of those percentages are extremely difficult to attain and even harder to maintain for any meaningful length of time. Are they possible? Yes, of course. But they are very challenging for most people to maintain on a regular basis. And the hard truth is that the changes we make in life that are worth making are those that are sustainable and repeatable. If you can't sustain a change, why make it in the first place?

For example, I've never heard someone say, "I want to go from rags to riches and then back to rags!" Have you? Yet millions of people play the lottery in hopes of attaining a level of wealth that unfortunately most can't maintain afterward.

Rather than focusing on huge leaps, let's focus on something that all of us can do:

I want you to get 1% better at loving yourself each day.

I want you to get 1% better at forgiving people who have hurt you each day.

I want you to get 1% better at cultivating your coworkers each day.

I want you to get 1% better at parenting your kids each day.

Get it?

What would happen to your financial future if you got 1% better at money management and debt elimination each day?

What would happen to your current relationship if you got 1% better at loving that person each day?

What would happen to your physical fitness and vitality if you got 1% better at taking care of yourself each day?

What would happen to your sales results if you got 1% better at understanding the demographics and psychographics of your target audience and prospecting for them each day?

Getting 1% better every single day is a shift that you can make and sustain no matter the current state of your life.

It's doable!

Five Ways You Can Shift Higher and Tune Up the Motorcycle of Your Life

1. There is another gear that you're meant to live your life from. It's simply waiting for you to actuate it.

2. There's no traffic on the extra mile. Go the extra mile each day in some small way and watch your life transform.

3. I am proud of you. Put your hand on your heart and receive that for ten seconds.

4. Remember that failure is not an option; it's a privilege reserved exclusively for those who try.

5. Each day you wake up, you receive a special invitation to get 1% better. Commit to bettering your best each day.

CHAPTER 2

Shift from Coasting to Living 3-D

We all have been guilty of coasting at one time or another in our lives. One definition of coasting is "moving but not being driven by the engine." Think about that. In other words, we go through the motions—day in and day out—but we are not driven by the engine of purpose, success, passion, and destiny—that inner desire to live life to the fullest. We've all experienced that. We will talk more about this engine in the next chapter.

Have you ever found yourself just coasting through life, in business or relationships, in academic pursuits or educational aspirations? Maybe you've been coasting in your personal development, coasting as you set and meet your financial goals or in your retirement planning. And we can't forget about coasting in your spiritual growth and career acceleration. Oh— and many of us are guilty of coasting with our health and nutrition. Do you have any of those "coasting" habits?

OK, Delatorro . . . stop asking!

According to the United Nations, the international average life expectancy is 72.6 years.[1]

So let me ask you a simple question: At the time you're experiencing this book, how old are you? For example, at the time of writing this book, I am 43 years young.

Based on the UN research, if I take 72.6 and subtract my current age (43) that means I have 29.6 summers left. Now you do it.

72.6

– _____ (your age here)

_____

Well, my friend, that's how many summers you've got left.

That alone should make you put this book down right now and SHIFT HIGHER so that you can start living more and enjoying being the best version of yourself that you can possibly be.

Some of you may have 40 summers left, or 50 summers left, but some of you may have only 20 summers left or 10 summers left to maximize and enjoy this thing we call life to the fullest. I have about 30 summers left, and I plan to live not just the summers but the rest of my years to the fullest!

If you knew you only had 10 summers left, how would you spend them?

- What trips would you take? And who with?
- What parts of the world would you go see?
- What experiences would you make sure you had with your family?
- What friends would you spend more time with?
- What old wounds would you heal so that you could be free to love more deeply and more honestly?
- What hobbies would you pick up?
- Whom would you want to attract into your life so that you could feel more complete?

We have to stop living as if we are all promised tomorrow, because we are not.

The adage says that you can be here today and gone tomorrow. The harsh truth is that you can be here today and gone today!

So the time is NOW! The next time someone asks you what time it is, tell them it's now o'clock!

According to the Worldometer website (https://www.worldometers. info/demographics/life-expectancy/), the ten countries with the highest life expectancy are

1. Hong Kong
2. Japan
3. Macao
4. Switzerland
5. Singapore
6. Italy
7. Spain
8. Australia
9. Channel Islands
10. Iceland

The same study found that women outlive men by between four to six years.

What's the point? It's time to live all the way out. It's time to roll the throttle and go for life!

3-D Living

We humans have never been taught to live life to the fullest. Think about it: Did you ever in elementary school, high school, or college take a semester-long course called Living an Amazing Life 101? Probably not. So how do we go about living such a life when we've never been taught exactly how? And going back to the Abbott research study mentioned in the introduction, just using the US as an example, we ranked sixty-fifth globally in terms of our feeling fulfilled in life. That's a failing grade, my friend!

The truth is that we've been taught and conditioned from the time we were born to live a one-dimensional, mediocre, status quo life. We were taught to coast! Be average, be ordinary, fit in, blend in, and don't make waves.

What if I told you that you've been lied to your entire life? May I prove it to you? As human beings, we are taught that the most important aspect of a person living a full life is based on one dimension. That one dimension is their *length of years*. Every year on our birthday, for most of us, we get friends and family together and do some form of celebration of our length of years.

However, I believe that to shift into a higher gear, get 1% better daily, and live life to the fullest, there are two other dimensions of life that we need to focus on. Those are someone's *width* of years (how wide someone lives or has lived) and someone's *depth* of years (how deeply someone lives or has lived).

One reason that we don't celebrate width and depth of years is that both of those dimensions are harder to measure and quantify than length. We simply look at a calendar and within seconds, we can use basic math to determine length of years. Width and depth are much more complex, as we'll discover throughout this book.

I love movies. Do you? I just love watching movies, going to the movies, and even teaching from concepts I learn in movies. And when I want to see a new movie, I always pay to see it in 3-D. I like to see the three-dimensional aspects, the width and depth, of the images on the screen; 3-D brings the movie to life in a totally different way than the traditional two-dimensional version of the film. You need special glasses to see a 3-D movie because your natural eyes simply can't process all the amazing elements that are baked into the film. And no matter how many millions of dollars that production studio spent on that amazing movie, you can't experience it the way it was supposed to be experienced without those 3-D lenses.

There is a life you're meant to be living. And I believe that God, life, and the universe are sending you plenty of action; you just need the right lenses to see it and experience it.

Haven't you felt that there was something deeper and more meaningful that you were supposed to be doing with your life and career?

Haven't you had that gnawing feeling in the gut that there's a wider world that you're supposed to be experiencing?

That's life whispering, calling, and eventually screaming at you to shift into a higher gear. My goal in this book is to give you a fresh pair of 3-D life lenses with which to look at, evaluate, and measure the overall size and substance of your life. We all know from mathematics that to determine the true size of anything, you must measure its width, length, and height/depth. In other words, there are three dimensions that determine size, not just one. The same is true of your life.

I remember when Marvel's *Infinity War* first came out. I went to see it in 3-D. Those tickets were expensive, but it was so worth it. Notice that I mentioned that the movie tickets were very expensive. I firmly believe that in life we have to differentiate between *price* and *cost*. You're going to have to pay a price to live life to the fullest. Doing so is not going to be cheap, and it's not going to be free. You will pay a premium to live life to the fullest. Most people aren't willing to pay that price, so they settle for mediocrity, for an average, ordinary, and downright half-cocked existence. But please know this: when you aren't willing to pay the price for an extraordinary life, you incur a significant cost. I'm going to say that again: there is a significant cost for not paying the price to live the 3-D life.

What could that cost be?

- Emotional peace
- Financial abundance
- Professional fulfillment
- Purpose fulfillment
- Destiny achievement
- Life mastery
- Mental fortitude
- Occupational freedom
- Interpersonal contentment
- Spiritual enlightenment

Are you willing to pay these costs, instead of paying the price to shift? I don't think so. The time to act and the time to shift is now!

Let's double-click on the "wide, long, and deep" philosophy a little more. I've been a traveling professional for about twenty-three years of my life. So I've been traveling for work as a speaker and author for twenty-three years (length of years). However, when it comes to the majority of the cities I've been to, I've just been in and out. In most of those cities,

- I didn't stay long enough to fully immerse myself in the culture of that city.
- I didn't get a chance to try multiple restaurants and signature dishes of that city.
- I didn't explore more of the surrounding towns and parts of the city because the airport and the hotel were where I was needed.
- I didn't get a chance to do exciting Groupons and other fun events.

I've been to New York four times, and I've never been to Central Park or the Statue of Liberty, and, as embarrassing as it sounds, I've never seen a Broadway show.

So, even though my length of travel has been impressive, my width of travel (traveling to other countries and continents) and my depth of travel (learning new languages, participating in a mission's trip or a spiritual retreat, staying with natives to better understand the culture) leave a lot to be desired.

Are you starting to see and understand what I'm talking about?

You could work at the same company for thirty years—a long time in terms of length of years—but never once experience a full career.

Did you experience the width of those thirty years in terms of taking on new projects outside your department's focus? Did you build relationships with people outside your clique? Did you participate in different philanthropic opportunities that the company provided or offered? These are all things that would have helped you live wide during those thirty years at that company.

What about mentoring? Did you mentor a new or struggling employee during your thirty years? Did you take bonus training that the company offered to deepen your skill set in critical areas? Did you take the time during lunches and breaks and outings to get to know your coworkers' personal lives outside work? These are keys to living deeply during that thirty-year career span.

3-D Living Personified

What do Princess Diana, Jimi Hendrix, Dr. Martin Luther King Jr., Chris Farley, Selena, Bruce Lee, Malcolm X, Bob Marley, and Anne Frank all have in common? These are all remarkable human beings who throughout human history have been considered to be transformational individuals in their own unique realms. Through their unique contribution to humanity, each one of these individuals goes down as someone who left this world notably different from the way they found it. However, each of these individuals have one powerful thing in common: none of them lived past the age of forty years old. Yep, even though their length of years was relatively short, they changed human history with their impact, influence, leadership, legacy, and profession. They were able to do this because they lived life to the fullest. They lived wide and deep.

Our society tells us that if a person lived until they were seventy or eighty years old, they lived a so-called full life. I would drastically disagree. I don't believe that just because someone lives until they're a hundred years old, they lived a full life. They might have seen a lot, they might have survived through a lot, and they might have experienced a lot; however, that does not necessarily mean that they lived, in my opinion, a "full life." Their depth of years could have been very shallow, and their width of years could have been very narrow.

I've heard it said that you can live a hundred years, or you can live one year a hundred times. Let that sink in for a minute. We have a choice to make every single day: Are we going to live life to the fullest? Are we going to shift into a higher gear? Living to the fullest means you must live the width of your years, the length of your years, and the depth of your years. You must live in all three dimensions. You must experience the movie of your life with 3-D glasses!

Jesus Christ is a perfect example of this concept. Now, hold on—this book is not about religion. However, Jesus Christ lived only to the age of thirty-three and a half. So he didn't live a super-long life; but because of the width of the perspective, impact, reach, and exposure of his teachings, and because of the depth of knowledge, wisdom, healing, and transformation with which he lived his life and helped to lead others, Jesus Christ easily goes down in human history as one of the most influential persons or deities known to man.

When was the last time you celebrated a happy depth day—to honor the depth to which you've been living? When was the last time you celebrated a happy width day—to commemorate how wide you've broadened your impact, perspective, and vantage point on life? You never see Happy Depth Day or Happy Width Day party photos on Instagram, Facebook, or Twitter, do you?

Please don't get me wrong. I want you to live as long as humanly possible. But just be clear that as you're living long, you must also focus on living as wide and as deep as you can.

Now I want you to think of ten people whom you admire personally and/or professionally. List their names here.

Now It's Your Turn

1. _____

2. _____

3. _____

4. _____

5. _____

6. _____

7. _____

8. _____

9. _____

10. _____

Nice job! Now, one thing that I know for sure about these ten individuals is that they were people who played full-out. They went all the way in. Whether it was a grandmother, someone in your community, a professional athlete whom you enjoy watching, a high-net-worth CEO whom you admire—the people on this list mean something to you. You might have listed even a kid who's overcoming health challenges in the hospital. There could be someone who, against all odds, has succeeded at a level that makes you want to be better. Regardless of whom you listed, the common thread is that they each lived wide, long, and deep.

They didn't half-bake, half-ass, or half-do anything. I've traveled all across the world, and one of the things I've realized is that all of humanity admires people who live full throttle. We aspire to be like people who live wide, long, and deep.

- We admire people who play full-out.
- We admire people who "lean in."
- We respect people who put it all on the line for their dream, their family, their beliefs (or yours), their aspirations, their country, their freedom and civil rights, and their greatest passions.
- We admire people who risk it all to manifest a vision that, many times, can only be seen initially by them alone.

If you cannot risk, you cannot grow.
If you cannot grow, you cannot become your best.
If you cannot become your best, you cannot be happy.
If you cannot be happy, what else matters?
—David Viscott

There's a big difference between living and existing. You could exist on the planet for a hundred years. Be born, exist, and die one hundred years later—still without having lived a full life. This book is all about helping you change that dynamic in your life. For example, let's take a quick look at last year.

If you're reading this book, you clearly survived the 365 days of last year.

You can think of the following questions about your year as hypothetical, but I encourage you to take some time and in a separate journal really sit with some of them and determine whether you're pleased with your answers. If not, it's time to shift into a higher gear!

Did You Live Wide during Those 365 Days?

- Did you widen your perspective on issues that you care about?
- Did you widen your reach of people whom you wanted to connect with and meet?
- Did you widen your vantage point by seeing a situation more than one way?
- Did you widen your beliefs about what's possible for you and those you love?
- Did you widen your lenses to see more in people than they can see in themselves?

Did You Live Long during Those 365 Days?

- Did each day count, and did each day matter?
- Did you get the most out of each day by planning your day intelligently?
- Did you get the most out of each week by working hard and playing hard?
- Did you lengthen your time with those you love and care about?
- Did you lengthen the time you had on vacation by making the most of your days?
- Did you lengthen your patience with an issue that you normally would cut short?
- Did you lengthen your stamina by not quitting on that business when you wanted to?

Did You Live Deep during Those 365 Days?

- Did you deepen your relationships by loving the people in your life harder?
- Did you deepen your impact by spending more time on projects to ensure a higher level of excellence?
- Did you deepen your understanding of God's word by studying scripture, perhaps?

- Did you deepen your business acumen by enrolling in some online classes or an additional certification or license?
- Did you deepen your philanthropic agenda by contributing to causes you care about?
- Did you deepen your emotional maturity by having crucial conversations led with love?

All of these are simple examples of how we can make the most of the years that we are blessed to experience. Each of us has a whole lot of living to do! Each day counts, and each day matters. Whatever you do daily, do it to the fullest.

The life that you want is going to require that you give it your all. You can't coast your way into an amazing life. You can't half-ass your way into an amazing life. No matter what you want, it will require your best effort. In my travels, I love to ask audiences what they want. I love to ask people by the thousands exactly what they want; what's amazing is that we all (regardless of our culture and creed) want the same things in life:

- Nice home
- Beautiful family
- Great vacations
- Good earnings
- Healthy kids
- Healing from the past
- To be loved
- Good friends
- Great experiences
- Contribution to causes we believe in
- Romantic love that's intoxicating
- Learning, growth, and self-development
- Healthy bodies that support us daily

Don't you see a lot of the things you want on this list? I sure do. In order to manifest these things so that they aren't just wishful thinking and imaginary craziness, we have to become intentional and purposeful, and we must kick our lives and careers into high gear. To achieve the things on the list, you've got to learn to shift!

Five Ways You Can Shift Higher and Tune Up the Motorcycle of Your Life

1. You were not designed to coast in life. You were meant to engage. Life is meant for you to actively participate, so get both hands and both feet involved in reaching your next level.

2. Just because you've done something for a long time doesn't at all mean that you have done it fully. Life is meant to be a three-dimensional experience. You're meant to live wide, long, and deep!

3. Think of a few areas in your life right now that you can deepen and widen. Whether it's your academics, parenting, romantic life, health, career, finances, body, mindset, or emotions—some area of your life is craving expansion. Shift . . . now!

4. Three-dimensional living also requires that you have on the right lenses to see your life the correct way and to process the magnificence of your life for all the vibrancy and multifaceted beauty that it provides. Change how you see your life, and your life will change.

5. Go back and look at the list of people whom you admire most. Write down three things that they all have in common. Whatever those three things are, consider how you can model those traits within yourself.

CHAPTER 3

Shift Requires Change. . . .
Will You Spare Some?

One of the most foundational differences between motorcycles and automobiles is that in order to ride a motorcycle, you must *accept the environment as it is*. On a motorcycle, you will be directly impacted by the environment. When you're in an automobile, the vehicle encapsulates you. It shields you, protects you, envelops you, and surrounds you. For example, if it's raining outside and you're in a vehicle, you're completely safe, protected, and shielded from the rain. The same goes if it's snowing, hailing, windy, sandy, dusty, muggy, hot, or freezing cold. None of the outside elements affect you when you're inside an automobile. And even though that's great, and it's comfortable, rewarding, and all those other wonderful things, the downside is that you don't get a chance to experience the environment as it really, truly is.

By contrast, when you're on a motorcycle, if it's hot outside, then you're going to be hot. If it's cold outside, then you need to wear layers because you're going to be cold. If it's windy out, you'll definitely feel that. If it's raining outside, prepare to get wet. To embrace living life to the fullest, you must accept the environment as it is. But that's part of the magic, the fun, the adventure, the thrill, and the freedom that come along with riding. You accept the outdoors for all that it offers, and you adjust yourself to make it work for you. This brings up a powerful leadership lesson that I learned a long time ago.

Either you proactively lead change, or you will reactively be changed by change! —Delatorro McNeal, II

Three Things Great Leaders Do

I believe that every high achiever must do three things if they want to lead their life at the next level. This is a valuable vintage leadership lesson:

1. You must see things as they are.
2. You must see things as better than the way they are.
3. You must make them the way you see them.

Most people are whiners, complainers, and procrastinators. But let's shift into a higher gear and become realists, optimists, and activists, shall we? Doesn't the latter sound so much better?

Step 1: See Things as They Are
(Be a Realist)

You must see things (just like the environment) as they are. One of the cardinal reasons why people never get close to topping themselves and living to the fullest is that they refuse to accept where things currently are. Rather than accepting and seeing their situation or circumstance as it truly is, they often want to put on rose-colored glasses. You've got to get real, raw, and honest with yourself about where you are in order to change your situation. I remember a time when I was in some significant bad credit card debt. I had tried several tricks to pay it off. But I had to take a brass-tacks honest look at my finances and make a list of my debts, interest rates, and balances. Then I was able to face my financial situation and make a real plan to change it. Today, I am pleased to report that I lead a life that allows me to be free of bad debt—because I followed these three simple steps. I know you're probably a positive, optimistic, and a good-hearted person, but if your situation stinks, you've got to admit that it stinks or you won't be able to shift it. Trust me, we aren't going to leave you here, but let's get honest:

- You must see your weight as it is. Even if you want to change it, first see it as it is.

- You must see your marriage as it is. Not as you want other people to see it, but as it is.

- You must see your net worth as it is, not the front you put on to impress people.

- You must see your money situation as it is, not the way you portray it on social media.

- You must see your business or employment as it is, even if it's struggling or no longer interesting.

Step 2: See Things as Better Than the Way They Are (Be an Optimist)

You must see things as better than the way they are. Look for the potential in your situation. Look for the silver lining around your clouds of doubt. Look for the open doors that your company's recent merger will create. In other words, you must envision things being better than the way they currently are. You've got to see a better picture of it than it the way it looks right now. This takes powerful foresight. It takes vision.

- See that rental property as better than the way it is.

- See your nutrition and wellness plan as better than the way it is.

- See your relationship as better than the way it is.

- See your kids' grades as better than the way they are.

- See yourself weighing less than you do right now and in better shape.

- See your personal life as much happier without that narcissistic ex–significant other you just broke up with.

- See your business with more customers and contracts than you have right now.

- See yourself happier and more fulfilled and more aligned than you are right now.

You've gotta see it as better than the way it is, which makes you a glass-half-full optimist. Most people struggle with this, because they suffer from "possibility" blindness. They just can't see a way out, up, over, or through. Therefore, they settle and then develop victim mentality. But not you. Regardless of your situation, it can get better. See it as better than the way it is.

Step 3: Make Things the Way You See Them (Be an Activist)

The last step is to make it the way you see it. Whatever you envisioned, you now have to make your current situation match it. Admittedly, that's much easier said than done, because it requires dedication, follow-through, consistency, and commitment, all things we will cultivate throughout this book together.

Now, to make your home the way you see it,

Or make your finances the way you see them,

Or make your relationship the way you see it,

Or make your friendship the way you see it,

Or make your business the way you see it,

Or make your career the way you see it.

Or make your body the way you see it,

Or make your money the way you see it,

Or make your wealth portfolio the way you see it . . .

. . . You're going to have to get off the nail that's causing you to compromise.

The Old Man and the Howling Dog There was a woman who was out jogging one morning. Off in the distance, she noticed a house. On the front porch of the house was an old man rocking in a rocking chair next to a dog that was making a loud howling sound. As she got closer and closer to the house, the howling sound of the dog got louder, even though the racket did not seem to bother the old man. She jogged up to and past the house to the continual agonizing sounds of the howling dog. After passing the house by about twenty-five yards, she stopped in her tracks and turned around to run back to the house to discover why the dog was making all that noise. Sweating, tired, and exhausted, she stuttered while asking the old man, "Why is your dog making all that noise?" The old man replied, "Well, ma'am, you see, he is lying down on a nail!" With a perplexed look on her face, she asked, "Well, why doesn't the dumb dog just get up and go lie somewhere else?" The old man immediately stopped rocking in his chair, pulled the toothpick out of his mouth, and looked the woman deeply in the eyes. He replied, "Well, ma'am, it's obvious that it must not hurt him bad enough!"

Ouch! How many of us are in the same boat? We have something, some issue, some challenge, some struggle, some problem in our lives that is poking us; and it hurts us bad enough to complain (howl) about it, but it doesn't hurt us bad enough to truly change it. Shifting requires change . . . but will **you** spare some?

My friend, it's time that you get up off whatever nail you've gotten comfortable lying on. It's time that you get sick and tired of being sick and tired and begin taking small but very assertive steps toward removing this challenge from your life. Your goals, dreams, and aspirations are on the line.

- If you're lying down on a credit debt nail—stop howling and start a debt reduction plan, get on a budget, and get a few friends to hold you accountable. Be consistent and live on a budget, and watch the debt disappear.

- If you're lying down on a mental health nail—stop howling about it and start seeing a licensed therapist, counselor, coach, psychologist, or psychiatrist and allow trained experts to help you combat the challenges of your past so that you can have victory in your future.

- If you're lying down on a career path nail—stop howling about your lack of passion for your current job, career, and/or business and start taking ownership of your professional happiness. Plug into work that fulfills you and brings you joy while you earn a paycheck. You don't have to cash in personal fulfillment for professional gain . . . you can have them both.

Keeping in mind the three simple steps to interpersonal leadership, think of something right now that you really and truly want to change in your life. What is one big thing in your life, career, or business that you want to change? Take a moment and write it down here, please. Once you write it down, I will take you through my six steps to changing it! Deal?

_____

_____

_____

The Six Phases of Real Change

When you are truly ready to make a major change in your life, you must make a few positive declarations that lead you down a path of progress toward your goals. In other words, you must not only believe these things but also decree your commitment to changing. As you make these declarations, you must also act on them on a consistent basis.

Step 1: It Must Change!

(Rewrite these words yourself here, please.)

_____

There are two words in this phrase that are very important. The word *It* enables you to identify the thing or things that must change. You cannot change what you do not confront, and you can't confront what you do not identify. You must define for yourself what the "It" is in your life. The second word that stands out is *must*. This word gives priority and urgency to your change. Far too many of us allow our goals, dreams, and positive changes to be optional instead of mandatory. As of today, be selfish and place positive changes at the top of your priority list.

Step 2: I Must Change It!

(Rewrite these words yourself here, please.)

_____

The word *I* is the most important word in this phrase. Far too many of us procrastinate on making positive changes in our lives because we are waiting on someone else or some other entity to make the change for us. Once you have identified the thing that must change, you must give the change an owner. And who is the most qualified? You! Yes, you must become the CEO of your change, correction, or adjustment. You are the chief execution (take-action) officer. The change you really seek must come from you. An old adage says, "If it is to be, then it's up to me!" Don't wait for anyone or anything else to create the change that you seek. It's not up to the government, the school system, the corporation, the church, or your family. If it shall come true, then it's up to you. Remember, the effort is up to you; the outcome is up to God!

Step 3: I Can Change It!

(Rewrite these words yourself here, please.)

Once you have assigned yourself as the owner of the change, you must realize that you possess the power to execute the change. You must believe with everything in your being that you can change your own life. You can change your situation, your circumstances, and your scenarios in life. You can lose weight. You can break that addiction. You can be a better parent. You can complete that certification. You can change your friends. You can go back to school. You can quit smoking or drinking. You can start and grow that business. You can rebound from divorce and find your ideal soul mate. Yes, you can!

However, my faith in you is not enough. You must know this to be true as well. Don't let anyone or anything convince you that it's your destiny to stay in a bad situation your entire life. Shift out of that stinking thinking. You can do it. You can impact this world. You can impact your community. You can take that step of faith and live your dreams. You can change the government, one policy at a time.

You can. You can. You can!

Step 4: I Will Change It!

(Rewrite these words yourself here, please.)

There is a big difference between what you *can* do and what you *will* do. So the next thing that you must affirm is that you will make the change. I hear many people talk a great game as to what they can do. However, the problem is that "can" is a rather empty term until you fill it with *will*! This is where determination comes in. "Can" is awesome, but it gives you too many options. By contrast, "will" gives you the chosen option. For example, when you go to a car dealership, there are many cars you can buy and many deals that the salesperson can do for you. However, once they pull your credit report, they quickly narrow those options down to what they will be able to do you for. I used to be impressed with what people could do. Now the only thing that impresses me is what someone will do. You must affirm within yourself that you will follow through on the changes that you want for yourself, your environment, and your loved ones. Get some fortitude in your bones and declare each and every day, "I will change it!"

Step 5: I Am Changing It!

(Rewrite these words yourself here, please.)

_____

This is normally the most uncelebrated time in your life. The process of change is normally very uncomfortable, and we therefore have the tendency to be hard on ourselves because we are constantly reminded that we are not yet where we want to be. However, I want to encourage you to take a quick look back and not only see but also appreciate how far you have come. You must affirm to yourself and others that you are changing it. You may not be there yet, but keep on working. You are getting closer and closer by the day. I believe that each step you take toward your dreams, God honors by pushing your destiny two steps closer to you. Begin to celebrate yourself even in the midst of your process. Reward yourself regularly at this stage, because the process can feel very lonely. For example, hundreds of people show up for the wedding, but few people are there for you during the process of building a successful marriage. Process can be lonely. Thousands show up the day of the big game, but during practice it's just you, the coach, your team, and the bleachers. Process can be lonely. Thousands may buy your books, but few were there when you were actually penning the words. Process can be lonely. But process brings provision, protection, and power. Those who abort the process miss out on the purpose of the blessings in their lives. Don't let anyone get you down. Why? Because you are changing it!

Step 6: I Have Changed It!

(Rewrite these words yourself here, please.)

Finally, you have made it. You started out with something that needed to change, and now you have changed it. Celebrate! Don't you dare achieve a goal without celebrating it. And there are several things you need to celebrate.

- Celebrate who you have become in the process of making the change.
- Celebrate those who coached you, mentored you, and supported you during the change process.
- Celebrate that you did not give up, even in spite of the obstacles you encountered.
- Celebrate that you will go into your next change effort armed with the momentum and wisdom you gained from this one. For example, the obstacle that you encounter on Monday teaches you a skill that you will need to handle the obstacle you face on Friday. Celebrate that the life lessons you've learned from past challenges are now your weapons to fight future struggles.
- Make sure that you let people know that you have changed. Many should be able to notice, but for those who suffer from positivity blindness, let them know that you have made certain significant changes in your life. And now that you have taken a tremendous step forward, don't allow others to pull you back by reminding you of who or what you used to be.

Do you see how if you follow the three steps that great leaders take to change anything and the six phases of change, you can gain immediate control of the motorcycle of your life and begin to take your aspirations to the next level? Because once you've completed these six phases of change, you haven't merely changed: you've transformed! Allow me to be the first to congratulate you on your new path.

Five Ways You Can Shift Higher and Tune Up the Motorcycle of Your Life

1. Just accept the environment as it is, prepare for it, and learn to enjoy it no matter what! The same is true for life in general. In order to make any real changes in your life, you must first accept and see your life as it truly is. Get honest with yourself.

2. You are a leader! And great leaders take these three steps: see things as they are; see things as better than what they are; and make things as they see them. A new day can begin in your life right now, simply by following these three simple steps.

3. What nail are you lying down on that's causing you to compromise and settle for mediocrity? Whatever that nail is, stop whining about it—get up off it and use that energy to change your circumstances.

4. There are six phases to the change process. Which one are you in right now regarding a change you're trying to make? What do you need to do today to move further in the direction of the next step in the process?

5. Always remember that, psychologically speaking, change feels like loss to most people, because it's a loss of certainty. So when you've made a major change, you will have to inform others around you and maybe even create a new circle of support because misery loves company, but so does greatness!

CHAPTER 4

Shift Your Focus and Put Your Weight into It

A **motorcycle is very different from a car.** If you want to change directions in a car, you must physically turn the steering wheel left or right; depending on how hard you turn the wheel, the car goes in that direction. But a car doesn't require much from you physically other than your ability to turn a wheel, which most people do with one hand while talking on the phone, putting on makeup, or eating.

If you want to go to the left or right on a motorcycle, you cannot "hard-turn" a steering wheel at all. Instead, you simply lean (shift your body weight) in the direction you want to go, and the bike goes that way. Period. But the bike takes 100% of its direction from the intentionality of the weight that you put into your turns. So to go left on a bike, you simply look left and lean left, and the bike goes left. The harder you lean, the harder or deeper the turn. The moment you lean a bike to the left or right, it's no longer centered. This means that gravity (negativity) is now working against you, and you must leverage the throttle (your action) to stay upright. We will revisit that more later. But the bike takes its full direction from you, and you will arrive at whatever destination you've put your weight into.

This idea begs four profound questions:

- What have you put your weight into lately?
- What have you really gone all in with?

- Whom have you gone all out for?
- When was the last time you "put all the chips on the table"?

85% of employees are not engaged in the workplace.
—Gallup's State of the Global Workplace

We live in a world where average is the acceptable standard. In fact, I believe that most people are not really alive anymore! Most people are similar to the Walking Dead. They are zombies—no life, but walking around simply because they haven't been buried yet. Daily, they're just going through the motions. Most people don't live life with a real sense of passion, enthusiasm, or energy. We've been trained by our culture to "do just enough to get by." Therefore, most people don't really go all in on anything. We live in a "just enough" world, and this keeps most people settling for ordinary.

It's been said before that many companies pay employees "just enough" so that they don't quit. At the same time, most employees work for employers "just enough" not to get fired! We are living a day-to-day existence of Just Enough.

If you're going to shift into a higher gear, you've got to get out of Just Enough land.

- Do you want to go to a restaurant that obeys food safety codes "just enough" to pass health department inspections?
- Do you want a lawyer representing you who studied "just enough" to pass the bar?
- Do you want to fly on a plane with a pilot who has flown "just enough" times to get their license?

Heck no! And why? You don't want to receive "just enough" service or products. You want and deserve excellence, and that's what we will focus on in this chapter.

In whatever area you want massive success, you will be required to lean all the way into it. It's going to require that you commit. It's going to require taking pride in all you do. It's going to require excellence.

I remember being a little boy coming home from church with my mom some Sundays, and a member of the church choir would have cooked something for my mother to try. We'd get it home, and my mom would heat it up and put it on plates for our family. And as soon as she took one bite of it (let's say its macaroni and cheese for the sake of conversation), if it was really good, she would say this one phrase every single time: "Aww, child . . . Sister Gallmon put her foot in this mac and cheese it's so good!" And she would start laughing.

I didn't understand why someone putting their feet into a food dish was a good thing. Sounded gross to me actually, until I learned that it was a metaphor. Basically, it meant that Sister Gallmon put her weight into the dish. She put her best into the dish. She put her all into the dish. She put her secret sauce into the dish.

With this and many other lessons, my mother taught me to always do my best in anything I attempted. And from that moment on, anytime I did anything well, whether it was performing in school or in a stage play or on the football field or in academics—I knew I had her approval when she said that I put my foot into it! That taught me to always put my full weight into the things that I go after in life, and this has served me extremely well in life and business.

1. If you want to shift your relationship—put more weight into it.
   - Carve out more quality time, go on more trips, have more deep talks, experience more intimacy, and discover more together.

2. If you want to shift your academics—put more weight into them.
   - Pick better study friends, actually go to class, and complete your assignments.

3. If you want to shift your body—put more weight into it.
   - Change your nutrition and meal prep, actually go to the gym or train for an endurance race.

4. If you want your business to grow—put more weight into it.
   - Value your customers, reinvent your products, learn internet marketing, and scale.

5. If you want your ideas to flourish—put more weight into them.

   • Get your ideas out of your head and on paper, find a mentor, and execute.

6. If you want your kids to grow up successful—put more weight into them.

   • Invest in their education, help them start a business, build their credit.

In the space here, tell me a few areas in your life where up to this point, you've been playing small, half-assing something, or just not going all in for something or someone that you know needs more of your weight (effort). Come on . . . you know exactly what I'm talking about.

_____

_____

_____

Thanks for your honesty. So right now, I want you to commit to taking a small step each day to get 1% better at doing the things you listed. Just something super-small and incremental that you can do on a daily basis to improve those areas in some small way. Deal?

Seven Keys to Cultivating the Weight of Excellence

When you begin to take the daily actions of putting your weight into things that matter to you, you will begin to cultivate the opposite of half-assery, which is excellence. Regardless of our industries, career titles, roles, functions, or positions, we all desire excellence in our organizations, teams, families, communities, and, most important, ourselves. If you were to ask most organizations what their top ten core values were, over 90% would probably list "excellence" in their top five. But how do we get to excellence? Is it a one-time achievement, or a perpetual, ongoing quest to be the best? As a peak performance expert, I've been fortunate enough to work with Fortune 100 organizations all over the world, and I've learned over the last twenty years that excellence is a habit.

It's a skill that can be learned. What follows are seven keys that I believe will help you—regardless of your industry or profession—to unlock that ever-elusive spirit of excellence, which will enable you to shift into a higher gear both personally and professionally.

1. Desire Excellence

If you want to be a person of excellence, you must first desire to be that type of person. A person of excellence doesn't take shortcuts. They don't go for the cheap things. They have a genuine desire to be excellent, and they have an attitude of not being willing to settle for half-baked, half-done, and half-assed results.

2. Find an Example of Excellence

In order to cultivate excellence, you must have an example. What does excellence look like in your industry? On your map of the world, what does excellence really look like? How does it sound, feel, smell, and taste? Excellence leaves clues—you have to find them, collect them, and follow their model (but put your spin on them).

3. Gain Access to Excellence

Once you've found an example of excellence, you must gain access to that example up close and personal so that you can see the behind the scenes, because excellence is 80% back end and 20% what you actually see. If you want to be excellent, you can't just sit in the audience and enjoy the play; you have to gain access to the backstage, which is where the real excellence is born. Sometimes gaining access to excellence may mean buying into it—investing in events, retreats, coaching, consulting, mentoring, experiences, and opportunities to spend time with the people you want to gain access to. Do whatever you can to gain access.

4. Serve Excellence

If you are blessed to gain access to a good example of excellence, serve excellence. Volunteer. Find a way to serve. Donate your time. Work for free. Don't ask for a single penny, because what you learn, you could never pay for anyway. As you serve a person or an organization of excellence, you will quickly learn that excellence is a Crock-pot process. There are no microwave results with excellence. It takes time. But if you have a humble and helping heart, you can serve your way into excellence.

5. Study the Details of Excellence

What makes a great dining experience excellent? What makes a great vacation excellent? What makes a car-buying experience excellent? What makes a movie, play, or production excellent? What makes a conference or event excellent? It's the attention to the detail! If you want to be excellent, focus on the details that your customer, client, or consumer cares about, and overdeliver on those details.

6. Demonstrate Excellence at Your Level

One of the biggest mistakes I see people make as they strive for excellence is that they negatively compare themselves with someone who has been excellent for thirty or forty years, and they get discouraged. Stop the madness. If that person has been doing something for thirty or forty years longer than you have, yes, they are going to be much better at it than you are. So now that that's settled, focus on being excellent at your level, with your resources, education, background, credentials, support system, know-how, creativity, and hustle. Be excellent at your level, and that will be more than enough for your tribe to love and support you.

7. Tweak Excellence

What makes people and organizations excellent is their commitment to continually improving on their previous level of excellence. Think about it: the root word of excellence is *excel*, which means to go above and beyond. As you do all seven of these steps to cultivate excellence, know that you will always be making changes, improvements, modifications, and adjustments to grow your excellence on a daily basis. Always remember that your best . . . is your next!

Put Your Wait into It

Remember how we talked about how a motorcycle will turn in whatever direction you put your weight into? Now let's focus on the second meaning of *weight*, but to do that we need to spell the word differently. To put your weight into it, you actually simultaneously have to put your "wait" into it as well. Yes, you must put excellent effort into the things you want, but you also must put in the time. You've got to let things bake in life! Yep, I just said a curse word. In 2021, I said a word that all high achievers hate, and that's the word *wait*.

The hard-core truth is that we live in a microwave, 5G, Wi-Fi, VR, Cash-App, Instacart, QuickPay, Instagram, Uber, InstaFamous, Lyft, right-now world. We just do. And most people don't like to wait for anything. We want what we want, and we want it right now! But what I've learned is that excellence, greatness, legacy, destiny, and fulfillment take time. There's no such thing as an overnight success. Every person I know and the hundreds whom I've studied who have been able to maintain their success for at least ten years did not have success overnight. It took many years of effort, many years of rejection, many years of blistered feet from pounding the pavement, and many bloody knuckles from knocking on the door of success to hit what we call "pay dirt."

You've got to learn to put your best effort into something (weight), and you have to give that effort some (wait = time) in order to harvest the success you desire. This is true of anything. No farmer plants a seed on Monday and has a harvest on Tuesday. No matter how much social media or fiber optic internet speed we have, success just doesn't work that way. There's a wise book that says, "As long as the earth remains, there will be planting and harvest" (Gen. 8:22, NLT).

Have you ever given up on something or someone too soon and later regretted it?

Have you ever stuck with something or someone no matter what and been glad you did?

You see, it works both ways!

I remember when I was divinely inspired to create my own reality TV show. Yes . . . I've been a big fan of business reality television for many years. In 2014, I came up with the idea to produce my own reality TV show based on public speaking. I recruited the best videographers, rented the best million-dollar mansion, hired the best coproducers to help me tell the story, and all that. In other words, I put my weight into it. But I also had to be patient with the process because from concept to actually seeing my show on Roku and Apple TV took 839 days! From concept to casting to filming to shopping for a distribution deal to crowdfunding the money necessary for postproduction costs to actually getting the show on air—839 days. But I sat on that egg until it hatched! Yep, 2.5 years. That's a long pregnancy, but it was so worth it. When you have an uncommon dream to birth, it will take an uncommon pregnancy term to deliver it. But I've created something that will exist forever because I was patient.

Be like a stamp and stick to one thing until it delivers!
—Delatorro McNeal, II

So many people never manifest their dreams because they don't stick to one thing until it delivers. Follow the metaphor for a quick second. Imagine if the postage on a package was animated. Now imagine that the $8.75 Priority Mail postage sticker could jump from package to package to package whenever it felt like it. Would the package that the sticker was originally placed on ever get from its original departure location to its ultimate destination? No, it would not. Because no package can get to its final destination unless the postage that's affixed to the package remains on the package through the entire process of delivery. We've got to have that same level of stick-to-itiveness when it comes to our goals and dreams. We have to have that same level of commitment to our vision, our profession, our physical health, our organizations, our family, our financial future, our kids, our significant others, our morals and values, our spirituality, our recreation and fun. We've got to stick to one thing until it manifests. Unfortunately, we live in a world that does not celebrate this. We don't really hear much about delayed gratification these days. We don't hear that much about sitting on an egg until it hatches. So we must supply our own intrinsic motivation to inspire ourselves to new levels of mastery.

Put your weight and your wait into whatever it is you want, and the goal you picked up this book trying to achieve is going to mandate your giving your best over a consistent period of time to fulfill and manifest your deepest desires.

Five Ways You Can Shift Higher and Tune Up the Motorcycle of Your Life

1. On the motorcycle of life, you will go in whatever direction you lean into. Therefore, you must put your weight into the direction you want to go—in all areas of your life in which you want to see a significant shift.

2. Get out of Just Enough land. No one successful lives there. Shift into a higher gear by focusing on autographing everything you do with excellence.

3. There are seven keys to cultivating excellence (desire, example, access, service, details, demonstration, and tweaking).

4. Be like a stamp and stick to one thing until it delivers. Persist until you succeed. Period.

5. Put your wait into your goals and dreams no matter how long they take. Sit on your eggs until they hatch.

CHAPTER 5

Shift from Excuses to Declarations, because You Can't Ride with the Kickstand Down

The purpose of a kickstand on a motorcycle is very similar to the purpose of a kickstand on a bicycle. The function of the kickstand is to keep the bike upright and support it when it is not in use—when it's not being ridden.

There is one epic difference between the kickstand of a bicycle and the kickstand of a motorcycle: on a motorcycle, you cannot even start the engine if the kickstand is down. The kickstand disengages the engine. It is almost like the safety on a gun. The safety on a gun is designed to make sure that you are 100% ready to fire your weapon, and it prevents misfires. So you can't start the motorcycle with the kickstand down, and if you've started the motorcycle and you engage the kickstand, the entire motorcycle immediately shuts off. There's a kill-switch mechanism inside that stalls the motorcycle dead in its tracks.

The kickstand on a motorcycle represents excuses. And you can't ride the motorcycle of your life as long as you're leaning on the crutch of your excuses! As long as you engage the kickstand (use your excuses), you're telling the motorcycle that you're not serious and you're not ready to ride.

The only time you need the kickstand is when you're parking the bike.

So follow the metaphor, please. If the purpose of the kickstand is to support the bike when the bike is not in use, then the only time an excuse should surface in your life is when you're not ready to ride. Because you can't possibly say that you're ready for your next level yet keep putting the kickstand down. Once you straddle a motorcycle, your legs do the work of the kickstand.

Do you want to live the quality of life you've always dreamed? If you answered yes, then kick back the kickstand. You don't need it to enjoy the ride. In fact, you can't use it to enjoy the ride.

Why People Lean on Their Excuses (Secondary Gain)

I've said that the purpose of the kickstand is to keep the bike comfortable and supported when not in use. Let me put that a little differently.

The purpose of your excuses is to keep you *comfortable and supported with your decision* to play small and not use your life to the fullest. Ouch! That one even hurt me, and I'm the author! LOL. But it's so true. Be super-duper careful with excuses, because they are very subtle, and they are meant to make you feel OK with mediocrity, average, and pulling back—not advancing forward with your life, career, business, relationships, health, money, family, or overall well-being.

Have you ever heard of the psychological term *secondary gain*? Secondary gain is defined as any advantage, such as increased attention, disability benefits, or release from unpleasant responsibilities, obtained as a result of having an illness.

Remember that the purpose of the kickstand is to keep the bike comfortably not in use or conveniently inactive, to help justify why you can't win and succeed. Always remember this . . . the thief who's trying to rob your house (metaphorically speaking) doesn't want you to know that he's there. What do I mean by this? Who is the thief? Fear. Fear doesn't want you to recognize its actions as fear based, but all excuses and all kickstands are rooted in some form of fear!

We will double-click more on fear in the next chapter, but for now let me finish unpacking secondary gain. With secondary gain, there is some positive or favorable benefit for you in playing small. It's that benefit that you love and become addicted to, that keeps you in an unfavorable position in life.

Let me give you an example of how this sucker works.

Let's say you're a busy, overworked, and underappreciated career professional, and you lead a busy family life. One day, unfortunately, you break your leg in a car accident. Ouch. I don't wish that on anyone, but just follow me for a second.

Of course, you don't like that you have a broken leg, because you can't walk; you can't do a lot of things that you're used to doing. You need help for nearly all the activities of day-to-day living. You don't like being helpless, and you want to get better quick, so you can get back to normal.

However, while you're recovering, the following benefits show up in your life:

- You get time off work.
- You get to stay home and enjoy your family.
- Your spouse does more of the chores you used to do.
- Your kids are nicer to each other and you, and cater to you.
- You collect disability insurance payments.
- Your family, neighbors, and friends come visit you regularly.
- You get to catch up on all your favorite TV shows.
- Your team at work takes up all the slack while you're gone.

Now, all these "secondary benefits" of your being "sick and incapacitated" begin to make you want to stay sick and incapacitated longer. These secondary gains make your "new norm" of being sick . . . very comfortable.

So the brain begins to delay your healing so that you can enjoy this disabled state and prolong it for as long as possible. That's why some people get sick and stay sick. That's why people sometimes become broke and stay broke. Because secondary gain is making their disadvantaged situation so "comfortable."

Here's the kicker: Do you really need a broken leg to get this love and attention from your family and team? Of course not. But that's what you think. And that's the issue. The truth is that you can get all the benefits—without the broken leg—simply by asking for what you want and need and being persistent until you get the affection, support, team spirit, relaxation, and cooperation that you deserve.

Remember, the goal of the kickstand is to make the motorcycle comfortable with not being used! Inactive! Kept upright.

We sometimes called this learned helplessness or a victim mentality. It's all the same stuff. This is why it's crucial that you not allow your excuses to hold you back from getting on your bike and enjoying the ride.

Kick back your kickstands! —Delatorro McNeal, II

Let's talk about the exact excuses that we most often use. According to the LifeHack website, these are the top twenty excuses most people make that stop them from reaching their dreams.[1]

- I'm too old to start.
- I'm not talented enough.
- I wasn't born in the right area.
- I come from a poor background.
- I'm not smart enough.
- I don't have the support.
- I don't have enough time to discover what I like.
- My family and friends don't think I'm capable.
- I don't know whether I will succeed.
- I've already dedicated myself to a different path.
- I'm just not lucky enough.
- I didn't have the right teachers.
- I'm not destined to succeed.
- I'm not motivated enough.
- I'm too easily distracted by other things.
- I'm not educated enough.
- I can't handle failure.
- I will start tomorrow.
- I'm not ready.
- I don't believe I can do it.

Check this out:

- No trip
- No jewelry
- No designer bag
- No high-fashion outfit
- No piece of real estate
- No investment account
- No second home overseas

None of these things are more expensive than your excuses. According to the *Inc.* website, here are the top ten excuses that unproductive people make at work. See if any of these apply to you or the people you work with.[2]

1. I'm overworked.
2. It's not my job.
3. I'll finish that later.
4. I don't have all of the answers yet.
5. I'll wait for my boss to tell me what to do.
6. I don't understand all the variables.
7. I don't see the benefit to me.
8. I might not get the credit. (Wow . . . now that's honest.)
9. I'm worried about the quality of my work.
10. I might fail.

If you really want to do something, you'll find a way.
If you don't, you'll find an excuse. —Jim Rohm

Ready to get rid of all of these whack kickstands?

There's a powerful psychological practice called *cognitive reframing*. When you reframe something, you take what appears to be a negative and find a way to turn it around so that you see the positive in it, allowing it to become useful for you.

By clinical definition, "cognitive reframing is a psychological technique that consists of identifying and then changing the way situations, experiences, events, ideas, and/or emotions are viewed. Cognitive reframing is the process by which such situations or thoughts are challenged and then changed."

For example, what if you stopped calling your issues in life and business "problems" (which has a negative connotation) and you started calling them "growth opportunities" (which has a positive connotation)? That one simple shift with your word choice makes a big difference and evokes a completely different response from you . . . doesn't it? Try doing this for the next thirty days, and ask a few friends and family members to join you in this "Shift Challenge." Email me at Delatorro@gmail.com and let me know how it went. I'm very interested to see how this one cognitive reframe can become a game changer for you.

In a *Psychology Today* article titled "Reframing" by Linda and Charlie Bloom, they say this about reframing:

> Reframing requires seeing something in a new way, in a context that allows us to recognize and appreciate positive aspects of our situation. Reframing helps us to use whatever life hands us as opportunities to be taken advantage of, rather than problems to be avoided. Breakdowns are transformed into challenges and new possibilities to experience life more fully and to become a more whole human being.[3]

I love their expression of cognitive reframing. So powerful and so essential to this book. I practice this skill of reframing every single day of my life as an entrepreneur. I am perpetually reframing the never-ending growth opportunities that come along with fatherhood, entrepreneurship, professional development, money and finance, faith and spirituality, relationships, race and ethnicity, and health and vitality. I'm constantly looking for new ways to see things and new vantage points from which to look at things that allow me to be able to process them more positively and productively. I intentionally keep people in my life (in the form of amazing friends, mentors, coaches, and colleagues) whom I run scenarios by, knowing that their vantage point will help me cognitively reframe how

I'm processing something, enabling me to digest what I'm experiencing (whether good or bad) in a better, healthier, and more productive, powerful, and edifying way. I call these reframed versions *positive declarations*.

So now that we know exactly what cognitive reframing is, let's close this chapter by doing an exercise around it, working with the excuses I listed earlier.

For each excuse that was listed, I am going to help you reframe it as a positive declaration. Each of these declarations will help you get rid of your kickstands, enabling you to engage the engine of the motorcycle of your life and live life to the fullest. But you must believe them in your heart, confess them with your mouth, and take divinely inspired action toward them.

- Old excuse: I'm too old to start.
  New declaration: *My past experience allows me to start . . . smarter.*

- Old excuse: I'm not talented enough.
  New declaration: *I am learning new skills daily.*

- Old excuse: I wasn't born in the right area.
  New declaration: *Geography doesn't dictate destiny.*

- Old excuse: I come from a poor background.
  New declaration: *As I succeed, I will bring others along and revitalize my old community.*

- Old excuse: I'm not smart enough.
  New declaration: *I am a lifelong learner and implementer.*

- Old excuse: I don't have the support.
  New declaration: *The right team is finding me, and I am finding them.*

- Old excuse: I don't have enough time to discover what I like.
  New declaration: *I know what I want.*

- Old excuse: My family and friends don't think I'm capable.
  New declaration: *I know I can do this; others will see it later on.*

- Old excuse: I don't know whether I will succeed.
  New declaration: *I am destined to succeed at this, no matter what.*

- Old excuse: I've already dedicated myself to a different path.
  New declaration: *I am multitalented and ambidextrous. I believe in multiple income streams.*

- Old excuse: I'm just not lucky enough.
  New declaration: *The right opportunities and doors open for me with grace and ease.*

- Old excuse: I didn't have the right teachers.
  New declaration: *Success leaves clues; and daily, I attract the right mentors to guide me.*

- Old excuse: I'm not destined to succeed.
  New declaration: *My destiny is what I say it is. Today, I say it's clear, bright, and in sight!*

- Old excuse: I'm not motivated enough.
  New declaration: *No one who succeeds does so alone. We all need support, and so do I.*

- Old excuse: I'm too easily distracted by other things.
  New declaration: *I work hard and I play harder. I focus now so I can have fun later.*

- Old excuse: I'm not educated enough.
  New declaration: *Each day I develop my mind with all the knowledge that books, people, and the internet can teach me.*

- Old excuse: I can't handle failure.
  New declaration: *Failure is an event, never a person. And failure is only feedback.*

- Old excuse: I will start tomorrow.
  New declaration: *Today is the tomorrow that I dreamed about yesterday. My time is now.*

- Old excuse: I'm not ready.
  New declaration: *I am more than ready to take a small step toward my dreams every day.*

- Old excuse: I don't believe I can do it.
  New declaration:*I believe in others' belief in me, until my own belief kicks in.*

Do you see how powerful cognitive reframing is? Notice how there wasn't a single excuse of the twenty listed that I couldn't reframe, and the same is true with your kickstands. Each of them can and must be reframed into something powerful, purposeful, profitable, and productive for you.

If you speak excuses, you will shift into a lower gear.

If you speak declarations you will shift into a _____!

What's the name of this book? Exactly. So you know which one I recommend!

My last assignment in this chapter is a gift. Visit www.ShiftIntoAHigher Gear.com; click on Free Book Bonuses, and you can download the PDF of all these declarations. There are even a few blank lines for adding your own positive declarations. I want you to print three copies of the declarations and post them in three places around your house: your mirror where you groom yourself, your refrigerator door, and the wall opposite your toilet. Then download the screensaver of the declarations and use it as the screensaver on your computer. That way, every time your mind comes up with an excuse (a kickstand), you can remove the kickstand by seeing and stating your declarations. Do this for thirty solid days with an accountability partner and watch what happens.

Five Ways You Can Shift Higher and Tune Up the Motorcycle of Your Life

1. You can't ride with the kickstand down. The only purpose of the kickstand is to support a bike that's not in use. Motorcycles, like life, are meant to be driven. If you make excuses, your life and dreams are not in use.

2. Secondary gain is what makes your excuses comfortable to you. Don't allow that to happen. Recognize what your excuses are trying to do, so that you don't play small and consistently under-perform for side benefits you can get in other more powerful and productive ways.

3. Create your own list of positive declarations and add them to mine. Recite them each day for thirty days straight with an accountability partner and celebrate as your life shifts as a direct result of this game-changing strategy.

4. Remember that your brain is your friend if you train it. Without proper training, your brain is always trying to make you comfortable with your decisions, whether growth based or comfort based.

5. There is nothing on earth more expensive than your excuses. Get rid of the kickstand so that you can enjoy the open road of life to the fullest while you get 1% better each and every day.

CHAPTER 6

Shift from Fear-Based Living to Faith-Based Living

Every day there are two warriors inside you, and they fight to control your feelings, thoughts, and actions. Those two warriors are fear and faith. And the one you feed the most is the one who wins each day. Your positive thoughts and actions feed faith. Your negative thoughts and inaction feed fear.

In *The Karate Kid Part III*, Danielson and Mr. Miyagi are in the sudden-death round of competition. Daniel is getting beaten pretty badly by Mike Barnes of Cobra Kai. The entire two-hour movie climaxes in the last five minutes as Mike gives Danielson an unfair and illegal leg sweep that renders him almost disabled. The audience gasps as Danielson crashes to the mat in agony, and most don't believe that he'll get back up again. Mr. Miyagi rushes to the mat to see about his prize student.

With pain rushing through his entire body, Danielson pleads with Mr. Miyagi. "I'm done, I'm done, it's over, I'm afraid, it's over, I'm finished, I just wanna go home now!" Mr. Miyagi, wincing in his face, says to his student, "Cannot, cannot, must not!" And then he says fourteen words that changed the course of my life personally and professionally way back when I was a ten-year-old kid watching the movie for the hundredth time. (Can you relate?)

He says to Danielson, "It's OK to lose to your opponent, but *you must not lose to fear!*"

Danielson says, "OK, Mr. Miyagi, you want me to admit it—I'm afraid of him, all right, I'm afraid of Mike." Mr. Miyagi silences his exhausted student with a firm "Ohe-ohe!"

He says, "Danielson, your best karate is still inside you. Now is your time to let it out!"

And in traditional mentor/teacher style, he drops the proverbial mic, walks off the mat back to the sidelines, and stares at his student from a distance to allow what he said to marinate long enough for Danielson to take action. Around that time, his opponent, Mike, rushes up to talk trash to Danielson, basically saying that his karate is useless and his teacher is a fake. He continues taunting Danielson by saying three words that personified fear for me and changed my life again. He said, "I own you . . . I own you, Laruso!" Mike, who represents fear to Danielson, says that he owns him! And I think that's what makes Danielson mad enough to get back up again.

Quick question: *Does fear own you?*

I wonder what you need to hear fear say to you to make you get up and kick its ass.

We are going to hit on this a lot in this chapter, so get ready!

If you've seen the movie, you know what happens next. Long story short, Danielson gets off the mat and uses a special move that Mr. Miyagi taught him, gets the point, and wins the match.

Fear Is Our Biggest Kickstand

In chapter 5, we did a deep dive into excuses and how excuses could easily be robbing you of living the remarkable quality of life that you desire. But excuses have a dad, yes, and his name is Fear! Over the years, I've learned that fear is the biggest stealer of dreams, visions, aspirations, plans, and ideas. Fear is what keeps most people—all over the world—from living their dreams, both personal and professional, at the highest level possible.

I say our kickstand because I still deal with fear every single day. So don't let anyone, (no matter how successful you perceive them to be) make you think that they have magically found the cure for fear. Fear is in your DNA. It's like adrenaline; it's just a part of our human makeup. You can't get rid of the emotion of fear, but you can leverage it, and you can replace the fears that have held you back—with faith! You can, should, must do that.

Fear has gotten the best of me many times in my life, but one thing I've learned is that the feeling of fear and your body's response to fear are not the issue. Fear will always show up at your house. The real question is, will you open the door, invite fear in, and let it stay in your guest bedroom for hours, days, weeks, months, and years?

You can't prevent fear from coming and knocking. But how long it stays with you is entirely up to you. Fear is a bully, and it constantly pushes most people around. But not you, and not any longer. Don't let that bully in your house!

Trust me—any time you're about to do anything new, different, special, rare, unique, out of the box, or just unfamiliar . . . fear will show its ugly face. It will come knocking—bank on it. Again, it's how you entertain this guest that really matters.

I know a little about fear because for twenty years now, I've made a full-time living doing what people fear more than anything on earth. I'm sure you know that public speaking is considered by many around the world to be one of the top three fears that human beings have, and in some countries, such as the United States, it's number one. People would rather get in a car accident, jump out of a plane, be bitten by a snake, or go on an impossibly steep roller coaster than give a public presentation. So not only did I have to overcome my own fears to succeed in this industry, but I've also had to help many others do the same through my programs and courses. During my four-day Full Throttle Experience annual conference, for example, we dedicate an entire day, called Fearless Friday, to this subject. We delve deep into helping attendees identify their fears, and we use extreme experiences to help people push past their fears and step boldly into their faith.

During this time, I've learned some amazing things about fear that have helped me personify it, deal with it, and leverage it to propel me and many others to remarkable futures.

Seven Facts about Fear and How to Leverage It

1. **Fear's number-one job is to keep you safe.** Rhonda Britten taught me this. She's a remarkable friend of mine, and she's a regular keynote speaker at Full Throttle. She's considered a world authority on fear. She helped me understand that fear is only doing its job when it enters your life. Its job (according to itself) is to keep you safe. It's to keep you alive. Its job is to help you survive. Because without the emotion of fear, you would not know how to sense and perceive danger. We need fear to help us avoid danger, but we don't need it to keep us from success, which is exactly what it does for most people.

2. **Fear knows everything about you.** You've got to get this point. One of the reasons you need to study and understand the personality of fear is that it's been learning and studying you your entire life. It knows a great many things about you. It knows what you like and dislike. It knows your childhood, your concerns, and your dreams. It knows your weaknesses and strengths and uses all that it knows about you against you to "protect" you. But as it's protecting you, it's limiting your life.

3. **Fear is mentioned in the Bible 365 times.** Regardless of your spiritual beliefs, it's pretty interesting that in one of the most globally popular and best-selling spiritual books of all time, the phrase "fear not" or "don't be afraid" is mentioned 365 separate times. And there are 365 days in a year. For me, that's a spiritual reminder every single day that we are to starve fear and feed faith.

4. **Fear can be passed down to you from previous generations.** Yep! You could be wrestling with the fear responses from your foremothers and forefathers. Research suggests that there is a genetic link to how fears and phobias manifest.[1] So if you're going to get fear from your ancestors, also get the faith of your ancestors to counteract it.

5. **Fear thoughts are always limiting and based in lack, scarcity, or confusion.** One question that I am always asked is, "Delatorro, how do I know when fear is talking to me versus when faith is talking to me?" And my answer is simple: Fear is always trying to restrict you. It's always trying to get you to focus on what's wrong—what's not

working, what's wrong with a person, place, thing, or opportunity. Fear will always pump the brakes on the things you want. Faith, on the other hand, will always push the gas and roll the throttle and expand you, build you, edify you, and inspire you.

6. Fear takes many forms. Fear loves to disguise itself. It's trying to get into your house, remember, so it wears different costumes, hoping you'll open the door and give it room to hang out. For example, fear dresses up as stress and shows up in your life as stress so that you don't attack it with the weapon of faith. Fear also loves to show up as anxiety so that you welcome it into your home with no problem. Fear also dresses up as indecision so that you don't recognize it. When you can't make a clear, confident decision about something or someone, know that fear is underneath. Don't be fooled: notice that no matter how fear dresses itself, the costume—the disguise—is a less-than-ideal feeling or emotion.

7. Fear is learned behavior. This is very empowering. Watch this. When I ask audiences all over the world to yell out their most common fears, they give me a flip chart full of stuff. Collectively they name about twenty-five to thirty different fears. Which is awesome. Then I tell the audience that it's a medical fact that as human beings, we were given only two fears at birth. And what's funny is that in 95% of audiences, they never name those two biological fears—the fear of falling and the fear of loud noises. Just those two. All other fears are what we call learned behavior. In other words, somewhere along your journey, you were taught to fear rejection or public speaking or success or failure or popularity or spiders or roller coasters or whatever. Here's the powerful part: if you can learn fear, you can also learn faith:

- Faith in your dreams
- Faith in your talents
- Faith in your future
- Faith in mentors
- Faith in your beliefs

- Faith in yourself
- Faith in your ideas
- Faith in your business acumen
- Faith in your goals
- Faith in your partner
- Faith in your children
- Faith in your growth and development
- Faith in your friends

I want to give you so much information about fear and faith that you'll be able to navigate in life and business and succeed in spite of how fear tries to show up.

Top Ten Fears That Hold People Back

We talked about cognitive reframing, but I want to show you how it works with fear just as well as it works with excuses.

Amy Morin, a licensed clinical social worker, psychotherapist, and author, wrote an article in *Psychology Today* reporting research that shows the top ten fears that hold most people back from the success they desire and deserve.[2]

1. **Change.** Change is good when your mindset toward it is great.
2. **Loneliness.** Invite yourself places; join groups, communities, and clubs and organizations.
3. **Failure.** You're going to fail on the way to something big or small, so go big!
4. **Rejection.** To paraphrase John Fuhrman, When someone tells you no, that just means you should say "Next![3]
5. **Uncertainty.** Learn to embrace the wisdom of the unknown and allow it to flow into your life.
6. **Something bad happening.** I've heard it said that approximately 85% of the things we worry about never happen—at least to most people!

7. **Getting hurt or injured.** Do all you can to implement precautions, while still enjoying the moment.

8. **Being judged.** People's judgments about you are a reflection of themselves, not you.

9. **Inadequacy.** All high achievers feel "not good enough" at times. Execute anyway.

10. **Loss of freedom.** There is a freedom in achievement that you can't find in mediocrity.

Fear is very slick. Remember, the thief in your house doesn't want you to know that he is there, so fear will frequently disguise itself in the details of your life that feel accurate so that you'll accept them. I think of this phenomenon as:

Facts vs. Truth

If you want to keep fear in check and prevent it from taking over your life, you've got to understand who is talking to you when you listen to the voices in your head.

Fear wants you to focus on the facts. Faith wants you to focus on the truth.

- Your fact might be that you have only $500 in the bank.
  The truth is that you have a million-dollar idea that, if you act on it, will produce wealth in your accounts soon.

- Your fact might be that you've been married and divorced and feel as though you can't get love right.
  The truth is that you're an amazing person, you've learned some valuable lessons, and your divine love will show up if you believe it and attract it.

- Your fact might be that you just moved to a new city, are slightly introverted, and feel as though you'll never meet friends.
  The truth is that you're an incredible friend, and with the right social engagement strategies, social apps, and intentional attendance at the right gatherings, you could be more popular than ever.

Do you get the point? You have to separate facts (which fear uses to discredit and disqualify you) from truth (which faith uses to edify, motivate, and inspire you).

So the next time you start to doubt yourself regarding how you feel about something, ask yourself, "Right now, am I listening to the facts of my situation, or am I listening to the truth of my situation?"

And you will know the truth,
and the truth will set you free. —John 8:32, NLT

So . . . What Are Your Fears?

Here is your chance to actuate some of this amazing content and put yourself in the victory position in your life. I want you to list ten fears that you struggle with and how you respond to those fears. Please be as specific as possible. Here are some examples:

- I am afraid of drowning, so I don't get in pools or go to beaches.
- I am afraid of wild animals, so I don't go to parks, zoos, or theme parks.
- I am afraid of being hurt again, so I don't commit to romantic relationships.

Now It's Your Turn

1. _____

2. _____

3. _____

4. _____

5. _____

6. _____

7. _____

8. _____

9. _____

10. _____

Yay! Great job! I am so proud of you, because we can't conquer what we don't confront, and we can't confront what we don't first identify. By making this list, you've taken a huge step toward turning fear into faith by giving your fears a name.

The Cure—Take Imperfect Action (the CIA)

I am going to talk about the components of a motorcycle in chapter 10, but for now, I need you to think about fear and faith like this: fear is the brakes on the motorcycle of your life, and faith is the throttle. Faith will always propel you forward and cause you to take action. Fear will always restrict you and cause you to slow down, totally stop, and sometimes never even get started.

I've learned that the number-one cure for the fears on your list is to take action. But not just any action. It has to be *consistent and imperfect action* (CIA). Hence the "1% better" conversation in chapter 1, remember?

Can you take massive action? YES! Rock out. Do that if you feel led, but the problem with massive action is that most people don't sustain it over a long period of time. So they take massive action for a moment, get a result, and then stop taking action, get lazy and/or complacent, and have to start all over again—because the result didn't stick. Sound familiar? It happens all the time with weight loss, money, relationships, careers, and physical and emotional well-being. So I recommend that rather than taking massive action once or twice, you combat your fears by taking consistent baby steps that are imperfect! By now, you should be asking yourself why I am making such a big deal about the concept of imperfect action. I am so glad you asked.

You are a high achiever. I've spent my entire life hanging around and inspiring high achievers. High achievers love to take action, but also love to procrastinate on said actions until they can do them perfectly. Perfectionism is a huge issue that keeps most high achievers from attacking their goals and dreams as they should. So I say take imperfect action, because we live in a world where companies release imperfect products all the time and we buy them left and right, but we wait to put our greatness out into the world . . . trying to be perfect.

For example, let's take the cell phone you have right now. Regardless of the company or brand, one thing I know with mathematical exactitude is that the manufacturer sold you that phone in imperfect condition. Why? Because the software that runs the phone has to be constantly updated. The apps you put on that phone have to be constantly updated, and every year a new version of the phone itself comes out, making the version you have obsolete. So simply by having enough faith to take imperfect action, the manufacturer created an imperfect product, marketed it to you, sold it to you in its imperfect state, made you install all the updates, made you buy the upgrades and accessories—all while using your money to fund its profits, bonuses, payroll, and continued research and development. Now that's some gangster business. And it happens every day, all the time, all around the world. So take consistent imperfect action—CIA. In other words, be like a helicopter. Take off from where you are and make adjustments in the air as you fly.

What Happened When I Made the Shift from Fear to Faith

Undoubtedly, you can and will live your dreams, manifest your vision board, top yourself consistently, and live life to the fullest. You simply must shift into a higher gear by starving your fears and feeding your faith.

- Growing up, I was afraid to get long parts in the church play because it was a lot of pressure to memorize all those lines.
  - Because I fed my faith, I became one of the most articulate and confident kids in my church, and performing developed a powerful skill within me to speak and present that I still use to this day.
- When I got to college, I wanted nothing more than to pledge a fraternity, but I was afraid of the process because I didn't want to be hazed or mistreated.
  - Because I fed my faith, I tried out for the fraternity. I didn't get accepted, and that was the best thing that could have happened to me, because although I was devastated initially, that rejection propelled me into student leadership, and I became one of the most respected student leaders on campus.

- I remember my second year working full-time at a preeminent university at the age of twenty-two while I was building my speaking career part-time. The time came for me to make the decision to quit that job and pursue my speaking career full-time. I was very afraid to take that leap of faith, because I knew that once I left, I would never again work at the university, nor would I ever work another "job" anymore. I was scared to death!

    o However, I fed my faith and took consistent imperfect action (CIA) toward developing my speaking business, surrounding myself with the right mentors and coaches. I spoke for every organization I could. I joined both Toastmasters and the National Speakers Association, and fifteen years later . . . I've written eight books, delivered over four thousand paid talks around the world, and am considered one of the best in my industry.

I could do this all day. The point is exactly the same ever time.

Feel the fear, but don't feed your fears. Feel the fear and feed your faith with action, and roll the throttle! If you do that, you will live a kickass life . . . on your terms!

Reframe Your Fear List into an Imperfect Action Faith List

Here is your chance to actuate this content and get in the victory position in your life. I want you to list ten faith declarations to replace the statements you expressed earlier. Then begin to speak them out loud on a daily basis. Here are some examples:

- I will take a six-week swim class at the YMCA so that I can enjoy pools and beaches.
- Mother nature is beautiful, and park rangers keep me safe, so I can enjoy parks.
- I deserve an amazing, loving romantic relationship, and when I find it, I'm all in!

Now It's Your Turn

1. _____

2. _____

3. _____

4. _____

5. _____

6. _____

7. _____

8. _____

9. _____

10. _____

Five Ways You Can Shift Higher and Tune Up the Motorcycle of Your Life

1. It's OK to lose to your opponent, but you must not lose to fear. If fear is the reason you are not executing on your dreams, replace your fear responses with faith responses.

2. Fear's number-one job is to keep you safe. It's just doing its job. Let it go work for someone else! Yes, let fear keep you from imminent danger, but not your important dreams. There's an epic difference.

3. The voice of fear is always restrictive (the brakes on your bike). The voice of faith is always expansive (the throttle on your bike)

4. Each day that you live, there are two warriors inside you, fear and faith. And the warrior that wins the day is always the one that you fed the most. You feed fear with procrastination, worry, anxiety, doubt, and inaction. You feed faith with affirmations, declarations, action, positive thinking, learning new skills, and leveling up your life regardless of your resources.

5. The cure for fear is to take consistent imperfect action (CIA). Yep, call the CIA on your fears, and they will disappear!

CHAPTER 7

Shift from Task Mastery to Emotional Mastery

The world we live in teaches us to achieve and achieve so that one day we will be "happy." I challenge you to shift that. Why not "happily achieve" so that you're not delaying the emotion you desire just for the sake of accomplishing a goal?

What My Mom Taught Me about Emotions

My mother passed away April 30, 2013, 5:30 p.m. EST at the ripe age of sixty-seven years young.

Her name was Olivia B. McNeal. She was far more than a parent. My mother was a mentor, teacher, coach, and advocate. By the time I was four years old, she had unknowingly started to groom me to do exactly what I'm doing right now. My mom had a remarkable gift for oratory, diction, enunciation, and pronunciation, and a very powerful command of the English language. That was my mother's greatest gift. Anybody who knew Olivia knew that she was probably one of the most well-spoken individuals you could ever meet. However, my mother was never a famous internationally renowned speaker, itinerant preacher, or well-known international brand or icon. She was simply a sensational communicator. And anytime you asked my mother how she was doing, she had one phrase she would always respond with: "Aww, child . . . I'm blessed." Those four words have been ingrained into my DNA for over forty-three years.

No matter what trials, tribulations, storms, issues, financial woes, relational disappointments, or uncertainties that came my mother's way, anytime you asked her how she was doing, her response was always the same "Aww, child . . . I'm blessed."

Unknowingly, my mother taught me one of the greatest lessons we can learn if we're going to shift into a higher gear; that lesson is that we must master our emotional states.

The Engine of Your Life

I believe that the engine of the motorcycle of life, the heartbeat of life, is our emotions, and it's how we master and manage our emotions on a daily basis that will determine whether we improve every single day, whether we shift into that next gear that we know is possible in any area of our lives, and whether or not we ultimately live an amazing, fulfilling, joyful life.

When I travel and speak, I ask audiences to do a simple activity to teach a profound lesson. I ask them to point to themselves, and all over the world, no matter whether the audience is five hundred people, five thousand people, or fifty thousand people, the number-one part of their anatomy that they always point to is not their head, not their skull, not their knees, not their buttocks, not their feet, not their ankles, not their abs (no matter how visible or invisible they are), and not their stomach. It's their heart. No matter where I am, when people point to the essence of who they are, they all agree that who they are is at the heart level. This begs dialogue and dissection—we must understand that the true engine of our lives is not our intellect but our emotions, and if we want to live life to the fullest, we must master our emotional states.

Do me a favor: please list the top ten emotions that you experience on a daily basis. Don't overthink this; just list them. Don't judge them or evaluate them. Just jot them down—no matter what they are.

1. _____

2. _____

3. _____

4. _____

5. _____

6. _____

7. _____

8. _____

9. _____

10. _____

Nice work! Very good! Isn't it kind of cool to see a list of the emotions that run through you every day? It's helpful to actually see them rather than just feel them.

Where Is Your Emotional Home?

Did you know that there are basically eight core human emotions that we experience on a day-to-day basis? And countless variations and nuances of those emotions that we as human beings experience? The eight basic emotions are joy, sadness, fear, disgust, surprise, anticipation, anger, and trust. There are many different models and frameworks identifying the basic ones; this list comes from a scientist named Robert Plutchik, who also created a wheel of emotions to illustrate these emotions in a compelling way. The wheel illustrates the dynamism of emotions, such as what happens to an emotion when it's left unchecked, is taken to the extreme, or is given too much wiggle room, and what you get when you combine two emotions, such as anticipation and joy.[1]

By definition, emotions are electrochemical signals that flow through us in an unending cycle. They are released in our brains in response to our perceptions of the world. I think that this is super interesting. Even though we often label them as good or bad, emotions themselves are inherently neutral. Their job is to give us signals on how to survive and thrive. The more enlightened we are about our emotions, the more we can learn how to appreciate all of them and the messages they are trying to send us, so that we can lead and navigate more fulfilling lives.

What navigational app do you use? I use the Waze app on my phone. No matter where I am, whether I'm on my motorcycle or in my truck or in a rental car, Waze can always navigate me back home. In fact, my home address is saved in the Waze app, so all I have to do is hit Home, and Waze navigates me there. With mathematical exactitude regardless of traffic, accidents, or construction, Waze always guides me back home. What's my point?

I firmly believe that you and I will always find our way back home— emotionally. You'll always find your way back to what's most comfortable for you. Your emotional safe haven. Whatever your core, most-dominant emotions are, you will find a way back to those on a daily basis.

Have you ever known someone who is self-absorbed, narcissistic, and all about themselves? No matter what the topic of conversation, they always find a way to make the focus somehow about them? Have you ever known someone who is always angry? No matter how great a day they have, no matter how awesome work is, and no matter how great their kids behave or how much money comes in that day, they find a way to find something to be aggravated, annoyed, disturbed, or pissed off about? I certainly have encountered such people. This happens because that person's emotional home (or, if I can quickly borrow a baseball analogy, their emotional home plate), is anger, and if that's where their primary emotional home is, no matter what happens in their day, no matter what journey they take on the motorcycle of their life, it will always bring them back to the address of anger.

Conversely, have you ever met someone who is just a radiant, vibrant, and beautiful light? No matter what happens in their day or what happens in their life, they find their way to joy. They find a way to see the silver lining around the cloud of doubt. They find a way to see something good in the situation. They find a way to always see the glass as half full rather than half empty. That person's emotional home is happiness, joy, peace, contentment, and balance, and because that is their emotional home, they are always able to find their way back to it.

What am I trying to say to you? You will always find your way back home. The question is, what's your address? Is your address resentment, ecstasy, fear, exuberance, elation, fun, excitement, doubt, dread, exhaustion, annoyance, disappointment, feeling marginalized? Regardless of what you call it, every one of us has an emotional home that has been programmed and conditioned into our subconscious mind.

Daily, regardless of how your day goes, consciously and subconsciously you will find a way back to whatever your dominant core emotions are, whether they be (by your definition) good emotions or bad ones. A footnote to consider: most therapists and psychologists agree that all emotions serve us in some way and that there is no such thing as a bad emotion. There are emotions that put us in high and low vibrational states. However, most therapists agree that emotions are meant to signal us in some way, shape, form, or fashion. What if you stopped labeling your emotions and started leveraging them? If something makes you upset, ask yourself why you are upset. Figure out how you can be curious about the message that the challenging emotion is sending you.

Let's do another quick activity to actuate this concept. Until now, what would you say have been the top five emotions that have been your emotional home? List the emotions that you tend to find yourself going home to metaphorically on a daily basis.

1. _____

2. _____

3. _____

4. _____

5. _____

OK, great! Now that you've shared yours with me . . . here are mine. These are the top five emotions that serve as my emotional home on a daily basis.

1. Gratitude

2. Peace

3. Passion

4. Fun

5. Love

- Can you see how a global brand that influences people all over the world can come from such an address?

- Can you see how raising two beautiful daughters could come from such an address?

- Do you see how touching the hearts of millions through the power of television can come from such an address?

Absolutely!

My mother's emotional home was always "Aww, child . . . I'm blessed!" It was gratitude. No matter the doctor's report. No matter the financial concerns. No matter the news she got from family or friends. She just had an engine that kept purring to gratitude!

So the question becomes, do you like your emotional home, or is it time for you to move? Do we need to call the movers and bring over some boxes, tape, and a U-Haul truck so that we can change your address? Moving can enable you to shift into a higher gear emotionally and move into a much better neighborhood. You'll have much better neighbors (which we're going to talk about in the next chapter), you'll have a chance for your kids to go to better schools, and you'll shop at better stores and get higher appreciation on the equity in your home.

If you don't like the primary five emotions that you tend to come back to on a daily basis—if you want to change your emotional address—the time to do so is right now. Let me ask you a question: What are the ideal five emotions that you would want to experience as a part of your new emotional home?

1. _____

2. _____

3. _____

4. _____

5. _____

Earlier in this book, you learned that great leaders do three things:

1. They see things as they are.

2. They see things as better than the way they are.

3. They make them the way they see them.

Now that you've identified your current emotional home and identified what your emotional home could be, you now have to make your emotional address the way you see it. What are five actions that you can take right now—what are five imperfect action steps that you can take today—that will begin to shift your emotional home address so that regardless of what happens in your day, you always come back to the five emotions you just listed? What are five actions that you can take to proactively relocate yourself emotionally?

Action step 1: _____

Action step 2: _____

Action step 3: _____

Action step 4: _____

Action step 5: _____

Seven Quick Keys to Protecting Your New Emotional Home

1. Practice radical self-care. Pour more into yourself than you do into others, and you'll keep yourself safe from outside negative influences.

2. Choose not to participate in conversations and dialogues that are of a low vibration. Conversations about drama, gossip, strife, and discouragement just don't belong anymore.

3. Minimize the time you spend with people who don't share your new mindset and heart set.

4. Practice mindfulness, meditation, and journaling about your day each day.

5. Use music to instantly shift your mood. It's the world's number-one atmosphere setter.

6. Consider taking the right supplements, such as ashwagandha and others, that holistically help keep your mental and emotional states strong.

7. Move your body. Emotion follows motion. You will be amazed at how quickly you can shift your emotions simply by shifting your motion. The word *emotion* is made up of the word *motion*. Shift how you move your body and you'll shift how you feel instantaneously.

Become the Emotions You Want to Experience the Most

One of the most powerful things that I learned to do a few years ago was to personify emotions that I wanted to experience on a more regular basis. Maybe this is something that you can try and see how it feels for you. It has made a major difference in my life and the lives of many of my friends and colleagues who practice this method. I learned to *be* emotions that I wanted to actualize. In other words, I learned to stop wanting the emotion as if the emotion were some outside entity. I learned how to begin to embody and visualize the emotions that I desire to experience as dwelling within myself. So rather than wanting to experience love and having to go find love as if love were down the street and around the corner somewhere, I simply *became love*. Rather than having to go find joy, what if I said that joy dwelled inside me? Rather than having to go find happiness as if happiness were in a different state or a different country, what if I embrace the reality that happiness is within me now?

I began to practice this, and it permanently shifted the engine of the motorcycle of my life. In order to manifest this new way of being, I began to write what's called "I am" statements every single day. I got up each morning, grabbed my journal, and wrote statements like these:

- I am love.
- I am joy.
- I am powerful.
- I am enough.
- I am clear.
- I am confident.
- I am certain.

- I am consistent.
- I am in demand.
- I am well-respected.
- I am ecstasy.
- I am sexy.
- I am intriguing.
- I am provocative.
- I am genuine.
- I am integrity.
- I am character.
- I am substance.
- I am depth.

The moment I began to locate the emotions I wanted to experience within myself and to consistently affirm them on a daily basis with passion, conviction, and consistency, I eventually became the very emotions that I previously thought existed elsewhere.

Make Gratitude Your Ace!

I believe that we as human beings are blessed with one singular emotion that has veto power over all the other challenging emotions that we experience. That emotion is gratitude.

It is almost impossible to experience the emotion of gratitude—true, deep, sincere gratitude—and any negative emotion at the exact same time. You don't have to believe me; just try it yourself right now. Think of something that maybe you're angry about; let's say it's a credit card bill that seems to never go away. OK—have you got that in your head right now? Good. Now I want you to flood your mind and heart with gratitude, authentic gratitude. Try now to hold space for how mad you are about your credit card bill and at the same time how grateful you are for something you purchased with that card. You can't, right? Here are some other combinations that are nearly impossible to maintain:

- Grateful and jealous
- Grateful and pissed off
- Grateful and envious
- Grateful and hateful
- Grateful and spiteful

It's very difficult to hold space authentically for both types of emotions at the exact same time. Gratitude always wins. So I want you to begin to live a life of daily gratitude. Each morning, I want you to make a list of eight things that you're grateful for at the top of your day; and at the end of your day, I want you to make a list of eight things that you're grateful for in terms of how the day went. Let that gratitude be the last thing that you feed your mind and your heart before you go to bed. If you begin to "bookend" your day with gratitude, you will shift into a higher gear like it's nobody's business. You will get 1% better every single day, and you will live life to the fullest. The engine of the motorcycle of your life will purr like a kitten and provide you with many miles of amazing rides in this journey, this adventure, this experience, this symphony that we call life.

As we wrap up this concept, remember that rather than focusing so much on *what* you do, which is task mastery, focus rather on *why* you do it—the emotion and the heart behind the action—and you'll always find your way. Imagine how much more personal and professional productivity you will experience as a direct result of shifting from task mastery to emotional mastery. Your quality emotions are the engine of the bike of your life, and with quality emotions you can accomplish anything you put your mind and heart to. Why? Because "Aww, child . . . you're blessed!"

Five Ways You Can Shift Higher and Tune Up the Motorcycle of Your Life

1. On the motorcycle of life, your emotions are the engine.

2. We all have an emotional home. You will always find your way back to your emotional home. No matter how amazing life is, if your emotional home is toxic, negative, and self-defeating, you won't live life to the fullest on your terms.

3. Don't just let emotions come and go. Capture them. Write them down and get curious about them. Ask the emotion why it came to visit you and what lesson or signal it's trying to leave with you.

4. The word *emotion* is 95% made up of the word *motion*. Your physiology will determine your psychology. Motion determines emotion. Want to change how you feel? Move your body more. Go for a walk, run, swim, or workout. Remember that the more action you take by rolling the throttle, the more you release power to the engine of your life to propel you forward.

5. Bookend your day with gratitude for what you do have, what is working, how good things are, and who is in your life, and you will attract more of whatever you're grateful for.

CHAPTER 8

Shift Your Posse, because Who You Ride with Matters

The number eight is my favorite number, and creating powerful relationships is one of my favorite subjects. I love the numeral 8 because when you write it, you can't tell where the number starts or ends. That's why spiritually, 8 represents infinity. It represents *abundance, wealth, and prosperity*. It represents *constant and perpetual growth, evolution, and advancement*. It also means *new beginnings*.

Now look back over the words I've italicized, because I did it intentionally. Do these words correctly describe your business, personal, spiritual, and romantic relationships? They should!

Relationships should add value to your life, just as you as a person whom people relate to should be adding great value to the lives of others.

- Your posse counts.
- Your clique counts.
- Your crew matters.
- Your friends are important.
- Your associates are crucial.
- Your connections are key.
- Your peeps are paramount.

- Your tribe is transformational.
- Your entourage is essential.

The people you hang with matter and will determine with mathematical exactitude both whether you arrive at your ultimate destination in life and whether you actually enjoy the ride along the way.

It's time that you shift your relationships into a higher gear. I believe that there are relationships in your life right now that could be responsible for changing the entire trajectory of your life and career, but that you simply are not capitalizing on.

I guarantee you that there are people in your life who are simply waiting on you to "graduate the conversation." They could rock your world in terms of business knowledge, financial acumen, family matters, personal growth, politics, or health and wellness, but you've yet to tap into that aspect of them because you're currently having very surface-level conversations—how they're doing, how's work, how's family.

Have you ever had a conversation with someone in your life whom you typically would only talk about ABC with, then all of a sudden, something happens, and it forces you to talk or ask about XYZ and then boom. You say, "I didn't know you knew anything about XYZ!" and they say back to you, "Well, that's because you didn't ask!" In that seminal and singular moment, you realize that your friend is a much deeper, richer, and fuller vessel from which to draw than you previously thought.

What's worse, maybe you've needed something or asked a friend, colleague, coworker, or family member to refer someone to you who can help you with your need, only to have them refer you to a close friend or family member whom you already know, but whom you never knew they could help you in that way. Everyone seemed to know their capabilities better than you did. Have you ever had that happen to you before? Why does it happen? It happens because familiarity breeds contempt, and we tend to take for granted what we become too familiar with. Think about it for a quick moment. Whom have you become so familiar with that you simply take them for granted and stay on the surface with them, rather than going deeper? I know that some names are already coming to mind!

It's time to shift into a higher gear and graduate the conversation.

Your Posse Audit

Right now, list the top twenty people in your life whom you talk, text, and video chat with the most. Next to each person's name, simply circle whether this person is adding positive value to your life or subtracting positive value from your life. Give yourself five points for every "adding" that you circle, and give yourself zero points for every "subtracting."

1. _____ (adding or subtracting)
2. _____ (adding or subtracting)
3. _____ (adding or subtracting)
4. _____ (adding or subtracting)
5. _____ (adding or subtracting)
6. _____ (adding or subtracting)
7. _____ (adding or subtracting)
8. _____ (adding or subtracting)
9. _____ (adding or subtracting)
10. _____ (adding or subtracting)
11. _____ (adding or subtracting)
12. _____ (adding or subtracting)
13. _____ (adding or subtracting)
14. _____ (adding or subtracting)
15. _____ (adding or subtracting)
16. _____ (adding or subtracting)
17. _____ (adding or subtracting)
18. _____ (adding or subtracting)
19. _____ (adding or subtracting)
20. _____ (adding or subtracting)

If you scored 90 to 100, you've got a great posse; continue to cultivate it.

If you scored 70 to 85, you have a decent posse, but it could use up-leveling.

If you scored 50 to 65, you really need to replace half the folks in your life.

If you scored 0 to 45, you need a complete overall of your relationships!

How do you feel about your score?

What's your plan of action for increasing your score and improving your numbers? Because numbers never improve by themselves. Remember that. You must be intentional about growing your numbers in this or anything else you want in life or business.

If you want to go fast, go alone. But if you want to go far—go together! —Author unknown

Who Is Riding with You?

In a car, if people you ride with are acting up in the backseat, they may be annoying, loud, and even obnoxious—but they don't impact the ride, your safety, and your arrival at your destination. The polar opposite is true on a motorcycle. On a motorcycle, who you ride with is extremely important because everything they do, and everything they don't do, you feel it, and it impacts the weight distribution, your safety, and the overall ride. The person riding with you on the motorcycle of your life can easily cause you to crash simply by not moving when you move.

- When you lean left, they are supposed to lean left with you.
- When you lean back, they are supposed to lean back with you.
- When you lean right, they should lean right with you.
- When you shift, they should shift with you, because everything they do affects you! It's truly a partnership during the ride.

I have this conversation with every single person who ever gets on my motorcycle. Because I feel everything that they do and don't do with me on my bike. And if I feel that they won't flow with me on my bike, they can't ride. I value my life too much to allow someone else to make me crash. You should be this protective about your network and your connections.

Do You Need to Change Your Five?

You will become the average of the five people closest to you.

We've all heard it said, and research backs this up, that you will tend to earn within 10% of your five closest friends. For some of you, that's a great thing, because you have high-earning friends. But for others of you, this is the kiss of death, because your close friends don't earn much at all.

The point? Increase your net worth, first by increasing your network.

If you hang around five millionaires, you'll be the sixth. —Denzel Washington

The Three Types of Relationships—Mentors, Mates, and Mentees

I want you to intentionally recruit three different types of riders to shift your posse.

Mentors

The first riders you need to recruit are mentors. Mentors are people who have been down the road that you're currently embarking upon. They are more seasoned professionals or individuals who have wisdom and insight to help you avoid costly mistakes and get to where you want to go faster. Mentors also can do with one phone call, text, or email what years of networking can't do. So you want mentors in your life because they can help you reach your end goal faster and more powerfully. Ultimately, a mentor is someone who started years ago on the highway that you're on and can tell you things to anticipate along the way, because they've many times been to the destination that you're seeking. Leverage quality mentors in your life.

Mates

The second riders you need to recruit are mates. These are folks who are on your journey right alongside you. They started on the highway at the same time that you did. So a mentor could be the dean of your online degree program, for example, but a mate could be someone in your cohort whom you're taking classes with and completing assignments with on a day-to-day basis. What I love about mates is that they give us companionship for the journey. They keep us laughing, smiling, crying, feeling, learning, and growing along the way. They keep us entertained and engrossed in the process of achieving whatever we set our minds and hearts to. I'm not a political person, but this is like the "running mate" in an election campaign—someone who is right beside the primary candidate to help them achieve their goal of being elected into office. You need mates. Mates make great accountability partners, which we will talk about later in this chapter.

Mentees

Lastly, make sure you reach back and bring other younger, less experienced bikers along with you by recruiting mentees into your biker posse. Mentees are people who started their journey down the highway of success months, years, and even decades after you did. They are people who view you the same way you view your mentor. They see you as very successful already, and they just want to learn, glean, and receive from you. What I love about mentees is that mentees/protégés help you make sense out of the nonsense that you've gone through on your journey. For example, have you ever asked yourself why you experienced something horrible in your past? No matter how much talking, healing, or therapy you went through—it still just didn't make sense. But then one day, a young person or someone who is less experienced than you are showed up in your life, and you were able to download your life experiences into them, and when you did that, all of a sudden your "failures" and "setbacks" felt more like "life lessons" and "comebacks." And isn't it so rewarding, refreshing, and renewing to know that what you went through created a road map of success and possibility for someone else? It's powerful!

So I encourage you to recruit mentors, mates, and mentees into your biker club; that will shift your posse into a higher gear for sure.

Know Whom You Need . . . Now!

One of the main reasons we keep misaligned people in our lives much longer than we should is out of misplaced loyalty. Because we've known these people for a long time, we just keep them around. Plus, most of us prefer a known hell to an unknown heaven! It's sad but true. We prefer the comfort of familiarity rather than the discomfort of the unknown growth possibilities. What keeps high achievers constantly growing and developing is that they are clear about whom they need in their lives presently. They don't allow misplaced loyalty from the past to hinder growth in the future. And you don't either. Just because someone grew up with you or went to college with you or worked at an old job with you or went to the same faith-based institution with you years ago doesn't make them the ideal candidate for your future unless they continue to show themselves as valuable.

- At this point in your career, do you need more connected professional mentors? If yes, then know that and go pursue that!
- At this point in your spiritual journey, do you need friends who are less judgmental? If yes, then know that and go pursue that!
- At this point in your wellness journey, do you need more health-conscious friends? If yes, then know that and go pursue that.
- At this point in your parenting journey, do you need more entrepreneurial parent friends? If yes, then know that and go pursue that.
- At this point in your healing journey, do you need more nurturing relationships? If yes, then know that and go after that.

My point? Know what you need now, and go about the business of finding where your posse is and connect with them.

Here are fifteen places you can look to find relationships that can shift everything into a higher gear.

1. MeetUp.com
2. EventBrite.com

3. Facebook.com/Events

4. Your local chamber of commerce

5. Your local professional association for your industry

6. Your local Rotary, Kiwanis, or Business Networking International groups

7. Toastmasters International

8. The NextDoor app for your neighborhood

9. Your local gym, spa, or fitness/wellness center

10. Your local church, synagogue, mosque, temple or spiritual campus

11. Dating apps

12. The pool of your friend groups (Good people know other good people.)

13. Facebook groups based on your interests, likes, and profession

14. LinkedIn groups based on your interest, likes, and profession

15. Local, state, national, and international conferences and conventions

These are just a few of the places you can look to find whom you need at this stage of your life.

A Powerful Question with a Revealing Answer

I don't think it takes that long to realize whether you've got the right biker posse. In many of my keynote presentations, I ask audiences one question that helps them quickly reveal this answer. I ask,

"If I handed you $100,000 cash today to start a business, would you hire your closest friends to help you run and grow that business?"

Most people say no, hell no, or something to that effect. So my follow-up question is,

"Well, if you wouldn't trust your current closest friends with $100,000 to start and grow a business, why on earth do you blindly trust them with your priceless and potentially multimillion-dollar life?"

Ouch . . . you can hear a pin drop. Why? Because most of us just allow people whom we've outgrown to remain in our lives for years, for no reason.

I can honestly tell you that if I were given a large sum of money to start or grow a business, I would 1,000% hire, contract with, and retain many of my closest friends and colleagues to grow that business. Absolutely! Hands down! Why? Because I've chosen to have very smart, resourceful, accomplished, and connected friends . . . on purpose.

And I want the exact same thing for you!

Accountability Partners and Mastermind Groups

According to a recent study in *PR NewsWire*, nearly 80% of Americans say that they don't drink enough water on a daily basis to maintain good health and hydration.[1]

I bring this up because for many years, I didn't drink enough water. I'm still not the biggest fan of water, but it's necessary, so I drink a lot of it every single day. But I knew I couldn't achieve my goal of drinking one gallon of water each day if I didn't have some support. I needed an accountability partner. I needed someone who would drink one gallon of water with me each day. So I found my person and invited them to the challenge. Then I bought a motivational water bottle that breaks the gallon up into small, manageable sections. Then I took the bottle with me everywhere, and I checked in with my accountability partner about eight to ten times per day to see how their water drinking was going and report how mine was going. Those check-ins were always helpful. (To be totally transparent, I still fall short some days. But I drink a lot more water now than I ever had before, and I'm much healthier for it.)

My point? If you really want to go far in life, find some powerful accountability partners to accompany you on important journeys.

- I wrote the manuscript of this book with an accountability partner (one person).
- I started going back to the gym with an accountability partner (one person).

- I changed how I managed my business with an accountability partner (one person).
- I grew my retirement accounts with an accountability partner (one person).
- I learned to take more vacations because of an accountability partner (one person).

Again, as I said earlier in this chapter, if you want to go fast, ride alone, but if you want to go far . . . ride together! Find someone to "do life," "do business," "do self-care," "do achievement," "do weight loss," "do parenting," or "do vacation" with you.

Finding an accountability partner can be as easy as writing a post on social media about what your desires are and asking serious people who want to do the same thing to inbox you, message you, or comment. Once they do, you decide whom you want to work with, and start the relationship! You don't need a lot of people. Just the right person.

Can you have more than one accountability partner? Absolutely! You can have several if you want, and together form an accountability group. However, there's another term for accountability in groups. When you want to succeed as a collective, you really want to form a mastermind.

The Best Biker Posse Is a Mastermind

At my Full Throttle Experience conference, I break the entire audience into small groups and make them form small biker clubs with the goal of turning them into a mastermind team of support for each other during the four days of the conference. By the end of the event, these folks have connected in a way that leaves everyone transformed and bonded for life.

According to Wikipedia, a mastermind group is a peer-to-peer mentoring group used to help members solve their problems with input and advice from the other like-minded and like-hearted group members. The concept was coined in 1925 by author Napoleon Hill in his book *The Law of Success* and was described in more detail in his 1937 legendary personal development best-seller, *Think and Grow Rich*.

I believe that masterminds have three main purposes, and that's to

- Shorten your learning curve
- Accelerate your results
- Gain access to connections by association

For the last twenty years that I've been in business, I've been a part of about seven different masterminds. Each one of them have indeed accomplished all three purposes for my personal life and my professional success. Oftentimes meeting on a quarterly or monthly basis, either live or virtually, masterminds are extremely powerful for so many of the people that I know—and I'm sure they will be very powerful for you as well.

As an entrepreneur, speaker, author, and coach, I mastermind with people who earn more than I do, and less. I mastermind with authors who have written more books than I have, and fewer, who have sold more books than I have, and fewer. There is something powerful you can learn from everyone.

Seven Quick Tips for Creating a Successful Mastermind

1. Be in a spiritual, mental, emotional, and interpersonal space to show up to a mastermind ready to serve the group. If you show up with a "taker mentality," neither you nor the group will succeed.

2. Find four other like-minded, like-hearted, and like-industried professionals who want to add value and grow using a mastermind group concept.

3. Decide on the overall goal of the mastermind. Is it to invest together, lose weight together, build business together, travel together, parent together, do internet or affiliate marketing together? What's the overall goal?

4. Decide how often your group will meet (monthly, quarterly, annually) and via what platform (live or virtual). Make sure that everyone is committed to the meetings, as they would be to a doctor's appointment. Require it to be taken seriously.

5. During your meeting, give everyone equal time. With five people in your group, each person should get fifteen minutes of thought partnership from the group about their challenges, struggles, issues, and stuck places. Each member should also have five minutes to share what's working, wins, successes, and accomplishments. So, within two hours, each person gets their chance in the hot seat. Pro tip: Your group could decide to go thirty extra minutes and make each member teach the others some skill set—that only they in the group know how to do—for six minutes. So, in the extra thirty minutes, the group shares five mini lessons on five different topics.

6. Before you end the mastermind meeting, each person takes two minutes to recap their own biggest personal and professional takeaways, and they set a goal for the action they will take between now and the next meeting and commit to that goal verbally to the group.

7. Once you're done committing to your goals, you all mutually agree on the place and time for the next mastermind meeting and wish each other well until then.

According to a recent *Forbes* magazine article, developing and participating in a mastermind can be one of the most important power moves you can make in your life and business. It will completely shift everything you're doing into a higher gear. Here are some of the benefits that masterminds can provide:[2]

- Accountability
- Regular connection
- Networks beyond your own to tap into
- A trusted circle of colleagues to help you make decisions
- A chance to learn from other businesses and leaders
- A confidential space to discuss challenges and problems
- A laboratory to learn and experiment
- A reflection of your own wisdom and expertise as you help others
- Potentially long-term friendships and connections

Your Most Important Riding Partner . . . You!

Remember this: the common denominator among your money, your career, your family, your goals, your vacations, your accomplishments, your kids, your wealth, your failures, your connections, your significant other, your retirement, your business, your physical health, and your personal fulfillment is always you!

You are the common denominator among all the various interconnected aspects of your life. You can't remove yourself from the equation; therefore, although we've spent an entire chapter talking about your relationships with others, always remember that the most important relationship is the one you have with yourself.

This entire book is about you, but again, I just want to highlight that none of this stuff (accountability partners, growing your five, or masterminds) works without you bringing the best version of yourself to the table.

If a biker can't take care of themself on a ride, they certainly can't take anyone else on the ride with them. Before you add people to the bike, make sure you are good. Be great at riding solo before you ask others to join. Work harder on yourself than you do anything else, and everything else will work out great!

Use everything I've taught you in this chapter to take the already amazing version of you to the next level, but please don't add these elements to a poorly developed you. It just won't work. For others to ride with you, you must first be a strong rider yourself.

Five Ways You Can Shift Higher and Tune Up the Motorcycle of Your Life

1. Since 8 is my favorite number, this chapter is a super-important one for you! It means prosperity, wealth, abundance, wholeness, and new beginnings. If you don't describe your personal and professional relationships using these words, you need to make some adjustments.

2. With whom do you need to graduate the conversation? You can shift into a higher gear quickly, simply by going deeper with some of the people you already have in your life.

3. You should be very intentional about developing relationships with mentors, mates, and mentees. If you want a successful biker club, add these three types of individuals to your personal and professional community.

4. The next time you want to achieve a big goal, you don't want to let everyone in on what you're doing. Instead, find one powerful accountability partner, and they will help you get 1% better every day on the way to that big goal.

5. As *Forbes* reminds us, one of the best power moves you can make in your career and in your personal life is to be a part of a mastermind team. Find your tribe, and together you all can take the road trip of your lives. Just wear really cool matching leather jackets, please!

CHAPTER 9

Shift into Drive and Avoid the Three Gears of Mediocrity

Cars are cool, but in my opinion, motorcycles are way cooler. Here's why. Cars give us too many other options from which to operate our personal and professional lives. One of the things I love to do at my Full Throttle Experience annual conference is invite someone on stage to sit on my motorcycle. Then I turn it on and ask them one question that impacts the rest of their lives forever. The answer to this question will impact you forever as well.

I ask, "What is the only gear that lights up when you turn the motorcycle on?" Then I hold the mic up to their mouth so that the audience can hear the answer. Every time, without fail, they smile and say, "Drive." A simple yet extremely profound answer. Here's why. A motorcycle only knows *drive*!

- It only knows *forward*.
- It only knows *growth*.
- It only knows *advancement*.
- It only knows *betterment*.
- It only knows *future*.

As soon as you turn most motorcycles on, it's already in Drive. There's no chance for you to go in any other direction but forward. Once you sit

111

on the bike and kick back the kickstand (which I already taught you how to do) and shift into first gear, as soon as you roll the throttle, you're going forward . . . powerfully and quickly. Ever notice that when a biker does have to back up for any reason, they have to do so manually? They have to back up with their legs. The moment they engage the throttle, they are going forward. Period! No exceptions! That's exactly how each day of your life should be. Without hesitation, your default direction and default gear should be forward.

Cars are set up differently, and because most of us live life the car way, we often don't get the results we want. So let's talk about the other gears that cars provide, which when utilized in life often lead to mediocrity.

Most cars have four gears, and these same four gears also exist in life and business: Drive, Reverse, Neutral, and Park.

Drive

When you're in Drive in life and business, you know it. You can just feel it.

Each day you experience forward movement, forward thinking, forward action, and forward effort. There is a momentum, focus, passion, fortitude, progress, leverage, zeal, and accomplishment that empowers your day when you're in Drive. Here are a few ways you can tell that your life is in Drive:

- You're working toward your goals.
- You're feeling focused and productive every day.
- You're working toward growing in your career and profession.
- Your financial future and assets are building and being leveraged.
- You're nurturing the relationships that matter in your life.
- You're trying new things that scare you.
- You're constantly reinventing yourself and those around you.
- You're destroying your comfort zone and living in your growth zone.
- There's energy, high vibration, excitement, and vitality to your days.

I want you living in Drive! It's a very powerful gear to live in each and every single day. This gear has an impact on all areas of your life.

But please allow me to warn you: just because you're in Drive in one area of your life doesn't mean that's the case in other areas. People have adopted a popular phrase that I totally disagree with. Many people believe and teach, "How you do anything is how you do everything!" I could not disagree more!

You can be in Drive in your parenting and be in Park in your marriage to the very person you parent with. You can be in Drive in your career, but be in Neutral when it comes to your personal health, wellness, and vitality. So just because you're in Drive in one area of your life doesn't mean that you're showing up like that everywhere. Let me ask you a question: Isn't right now a great time to shift into a higher gear in an area of your life that's not currently in Drive?

Reverse

In a car, we use Reverse to back out of our garage and parking spaces and also to turn down streets we missed. So Reverse is useful in cars. But in life and business, Reverse can be extremely counterproductive to your living the life of your dreams. We exist within time, and time is always moving forward. The most valuable asset you possess is not your money but your time, because once your time has expired, that's it. Your impact, legacy, and influence live on, but you physically are no longer here. We have to use our time carefully because it's extremely valuable and irreplaceable.

If you use your time to constantly be in Reverse, that means you're always going back into the "unchangeable" past to dwell. The majority of your conversation is about things that have already happened, events from yesterday. You know you're in Reverse when you hold grudges, bitterness, resentment, and even disdain in your heart toward people, places, things, and events from the past. Things that you can't change no matter how badly you may want to. You know you're in Reverse when you struggle with practicing "presence"—meaning you can't seem to live in today. You're most comfortable with bringing up issues from the past and using them as a justification, excuse, crutch, or reason for why you are not where you desire to be.

Now here's some major truth for you: most people are in Reverse and don't even know it.

Most people don't get over old relationships before they get into new ones. I was guilty of that in my past; then I took time to fix my issues with therapy, counseling, accountability partners, mentors, and radical self-care. Yep, I said it . . . therapy.

If you find yourself still upset over a boss who fired you ten years ago, if you're still bitter about what your ex-spouse or ex–significant other did twenty years ago, if you find yourself not trusting people because of something someone did to you three years ago, or if you find yourself repeating the same pathology, patterns, or cycles of destructive behavior that are not advancing your life or career, then you may need to see a licensed therapist—a professional who is trained to help you actually heal from your past so that you get out of that unproductive gear of Reverse. Driving fast in Reverse may look cool in the movies, but it's extremely dangerous and destructive in real life.

In what area of your life or career are you currently in Reverse? Always remember that when living the bike way, Reverse does not exist.

Neutral

Reverse is bad, but Neutral can be even worse. When you're in Neutral, you're without a gear at all. You're not attached to the transmission at all. You're just idling. You're not even under power at that point.

- Neutral sounds a lot like "I don't know."
- Neutral sounds a lot like "It doesn't matter to me!"
- Neutral sounds a lot like "Who cares?"
- Neutral sounds a lot like "Whatever."

Neutral is a very apathetic and low-vibration place that people often find themselves because of discouragement, disappointment, unmet expectations, and sheer exhaustion with trying.

You know you're in Neutral when you've stopped trying. You may still be moving, but you're no longer under power. As we talked about at the beginning of this book, you're coasting. You're kind of drifting along, like a boat that's no longer in gear and is just going in whatever direction the tide takes it.

What's dangerous about being in Neutral for high achievers like us is that we can mask being in Neutral very well, because we have charisma, charm, energy, personality, and success in other areas, which allows us to distract most people in the general public from our lack of superior performance.

Be very careful not to allow the challenges of life and business to make you indifferent. Because once you're too indifferent, you're in Neutral in that area of your life.

For example, because most people have tried so many diets and weight-loss gimmicks and tricks—most of which have not permanently worked for them—they go into Neutral in relation to their fitness and well-being. They are just kind of lackluster about engaging in maintaining a healthy body and a nutrition plan. Have you ever been there? I know I have!

Sometimes the disappointment with how our kids behave can cause us to become indifferent about parenting them anymore; we just leave them to deal with life consequences. Sometimes countless disappointments and bad experiences in trying to find and hold on to romantic love can make a person neutral about the possibilities, so they just say, "I'll just be single the rest of my life, because there's no good men/women out there!"

I personally don't know anyone who's crushing it in life and business who remains in Neutral. Being disengaged is not the answer.

Progress equals happiness —Tony Robbins

Park

I remember a time when not regularly using my motorcycle cost me about $400. Yep, I was "busy" working in my business as an entrepreneur, so I wasn't riding my motorcycle weekly as I normally do. One particular day, I wanted to take my puppy, Simba, on a bike ride, so we got on the bike and headed out to Epperson Lagoon in Wesley Chapel. It was a beautiful day. The ride took only ten minutes. Once we arrived, I parked my motorcycle and took Simba for a nice walk. When we got back and prepared to leave, my bike wouldn't start. I tried everything, and it just wouldn't start. The battery was dead. I was so upset, and what's worse, my cell-phone battery was at about 7%. I had to think of a strategy fast. I called my insurance company and reported that I needed roadside assistance. But my battery wouldn't last the forty-five-minute wait, so I had to call an Uber to come get me and Simba and take us back home. I got home, charged my phone, and put Simba in his crate. I then met roadside assistance back where my bike was stranded. The roadside assistance driver loaded my bike and took it to the dealership. The next day, I got a call that replacing the battery and a few other things that were wrong was going to cost me about $250 in parts and labor. In addition, because the dealership was outside the towing area, I got a bill for an extra $100 from the towing company.

A perfectly good Saturday was cut short and turned out to be super-expensive, all for one reason. A lack of use! The bike dealership told me that my entire ordeal could have been easily avoided just by making a commitment to ride my motorcycle for at least thirty minutes once a week to keep everything charged, working, and functioning properly. Keeping it parked in my garage was killing my motorcycle. The fact is, a motorcycle, a car, a boat, an airplane . . . your body, your mind, your life . . . is meant to be used, and when it's just parked and in a state of nonuse for days, weeks, or months, it wears out.

You actually do more damage to your life through inaction and nonuse than you ever will through consistent action and daily use. Read that sentence again!

You think that as long as you're parked, you're fine. Nope!

When you're in Park, your engine, battery, transmission, brakes, tires, gears, spark plugs, oil, and mechanisms get no action. And just like the muscles in our bodies, when they don't get consistent use, they begin to atrophy.

Let me ask you some hard questions, and yes, the goal is to get into your business! That's why you bought this book.

1. Is your romantic relationship in Park right now?

2. Is your relationship with one of your parents in Park right now?

3. Is your relationship with one of your children in Park right now?

4. Is your interpersonal leadership with yourself in Park right now?

5. Is your career growth in Park right now?

6. Is your business development in Park right now?

7. Is your spiritual growth in Park right now?

8. Is your financial portfolio or retirement plan in Park right now?

It's time to shift into a higher gear and get out of Park. Whatever muscles you're actively choosing not to use . . . you will lose!

The Cure

We've talked in depth about three unproductive gears: Reverse, Neutral, and Park. One of the greatest keys to getting out of these unproductive gears is *forgiveness*. Forgiving yourself for your mistakes of the past and also forgiving other people who have disappointed you and let you down. Because once you can forgive, you can begin to move forward and get your life into the powerful and productive higher gear called Drive.

The Benefits of Staying in Drive

We all know that in 2020, our world was plagued with the COVID-19 pandemic. It caused the entire world to shift into Park because of mandatory quarantines. During that time, many people felt hopeless and helpless as we experienced unemployment, record health care spikes, and financial, racial, and political unrest like never before. However, during that time, I watched with my own eyes as some people dealt with the COVID-19 pandemic very differently.

I noticed that these driven people found ways to produce in the pandemic and pivot instead of panic. Those people found ways to thrive and, in some cases, do better during the crisis than they did before it.

For me personally, because I am a very driven person and I stay in Drive in my life personally and professionally, I was able to accomplish many amazing goals in 2020. I had tons of reason and justifications to shift into Neutral, Park, or Reverse, but I didn't. As a result, I was able to achieve the following goals:

- Completed a certification in the Level 2 DISC Model of Human Behavior
- Completed my concealed weapon permit class
- Completed two levels of salsa and bachata classes
- Got a new dog named Simba, who's a wonderful addition to my family
- Learned new financial principles that put my company in a better place
- Paid off debt in my business and personal life, which increased my credit score
- Got back into the gym and started drinking more water per day
- Taught my daughters more about entrepreneurship during virtual school
- Pivoted all my live speaker training programs to sold-out virtual offerings
- Pitched the concept for this book to a major publisher and landed a book deal
- Wrote the entire first draft of this book to the tune of forty thousand words
- Cultivated personal and professional relationships through Zoom meetings
- Completed my Florida boating certification class

All of this within nine months, between March and December of 2020. These are examples of some of the many results that come into your life and business when you're determined to stay in Drive and live each day in Drive. I told you in chapter 1 that life gives you one open invitation every day in the form of a question: Will you be better today than you were yesterday? To better your best and live life to the fullest, you must stay in Drive!

Five Ways You Can Shift Higher and Tune Up the Motorcycle of Your Life

1. A bike only knows forward. It only knows Drive. Surround yourself with people who not only think this way but also live this way.

2. How you do anything is *not* how you do everything. Focus on shifting into Drive in the areas of your life that you haven't mastered yet.

3. Honestly assess your constant communication. If it's focused on events, places, things, and people from the past, there's a good chance that you're in Reverse. Consider hiring a qualified, credentialed therapist to work with you, because healed is the new sexy!

4. If you're constantly lackluster or nonchalant about your life or career, you're probably in Neutral, and you're drifting and spinning your wheels. Plug into something or someone who gives you passion, purpose, and positivity to reignite you and get you into Drive.

5. The number-one key to getting out of Park, Neutral, or Reverse is forgiveness. Begin to practice radical self-compassion by forgiving others and, most important, forgiving yourself for the mistakes and missteps of the past. Take small daily action steps to stay engaged and use the motorcycle of your life for the powerful purpose for which it was created.

CHAPTER 10

Shift Your Position to Shift Your Condition

I am convinced that most people sit on the motorcycle of life backward. I actually sit on my bike backward at my Full Throttle Experience conference to illustrate a powerful point. Sure, we all want to change our lives, but in order to really do so, we've got to make another shift. We have to shift our position to shift the conditions we often find ourselves in personally and professionally.

When you sit on the motorcycle of life backward, you have no access to the controls of the bike. The controls are located only on the front of the bike, so you have to face the right way. The front wheel of the motorcycle represents your vision. The front wheel is for steering. Your life will go in whatever direction you steer it in. It's in front of you, and it's a free-spinning wheel. There's no motor attached to the front wheel because most motorcycles are rear-wheel drive. Your vision, just like the front wheel, should be constantly free spinning, ever evolving, and always growing and expanding. You should always face your vision of your future.

Shift into Your Rightful Position

When you sit on the motorcycle of life backward, you're looking at the rear wheel, which represents your past. The back wheel is what's connected to the drive train, which is connected to the transmission and the engine. So when you roll the throttle, all that power is distributed to the rear wheel to propel you forward. Therefore, all of your power is really in your back wheel. Hence why most bikes have a thicker, fatter, and more robust back tire than the front tire. We all have more past than we do present, and the future (although it's free spinning) is not promised to us. What I love about the way a motorcycle is designed is that when you change your position and sit on it properly, you have direct access to everything—namely, the handles, the brakes, the throttle, and the clutch. What I love about the throttle is that when you roll the throttle—which is in front of you—it sends a burst of energy to the back wheel, which is your past and uses that energy to propel you into your future. Don't forget the past; just learn to leverage your past to propel you forward. Remember, a motorcycle only knows Drive!

The left brake controls the back wheel, and the right brake controls the front wheel. When I was learning to ride many years ago, I was taught that when you're deep in a curve, you always want to "drag the back brake," but you never want to "jam the front brake." Now go back and think about how that applies to life and business. When we are going through changes and challenges, we want to slow down on the things from the past that try to hinder us, but we never want to stop the vision of the future that we are working toward. And always remember that the throttle, which represents action, is your friend. Because when you're in a curve and gravity is working against you on that motorcycle, the only thing that brings a motorcycle back upright is rolling the throttle. As you give the bike gas and take the inspired action necessary toward your goals and dreams, you will pull out of any curvy situation that life or business hands you.

Leaning into the Curves

I've had so many junctures in my life where I was deep in an emotional, occupational, financial, personal, spiritual, or entrepreneurial curve, and I wasn't exactly sure how I was going to get out of my situation. Rather than panicking, however, I decided to lean into the direction of the curves by getting curious about what lessons my challenges and storms were trying to teach me. I leaned into my curves, put the brakes on the programming from my past, and, even though it was scary, I rolled the throttle and took massive action in the middle of the curves of my life, and that's exactly what has always pulled me out successfully.

I want you to think of something you may be going through right now, and ask yourself whether you're allowing your programming, conditioning, and hindering mindsets from past situations to have too much of a say-so in your ride. If so, hit the brakes on that stuff with your left hand, lean into the curve by asking good questions about the curve that you're in, and then, although it's counterintuitive, roll the throttle right in the middle of your curve and watch your bike get upright! I wrote all about this concept of pulling out of adversity in my sixth book, *Thriving Through Your Storms: 12 Profound Lessons to Help You Grow Through Anything You Go Through in Life*. (You can get it on Amazon or Audible.)

Your Rightful Position

The title of this chapter is Shift Your Position to Shift Your Condition. I need you to understand that your rightful position is one of royalty, leadership, power, and authority.

According to an article in *Forbes* magazine online, in 2019, Disney's *The Lion King* franchise topped $11.6 billion in revenues, making it the highest-grossing franchise in box-office history.[1] This announcement came during the celebration of the *Lion King's* twenty-year anniversary of screen and stage brilliance. People all over the world have been impacted by the powerful life lessons of *The Lion King*. As a professional speaker, I've been teaching lessons from this remarkable film for about the last eighteen years. I'm so enamored of the concept that my puppy's name is Simba! However, I can boil down the central message of that $11.6 billion franchise into the title of this very chapter. *The Lion King* is really about the importance for all of us of taking our rightful position in life as the "king" (this term is gender neutral) of the Pride Rock of our own lives. And if we are going to shift into a higher gear, we must sit on the motorcycle of life the correct way and take our rightful position.

We see this same theme of taking your rightful position play out in Marvel's global sensation *Black Panther*, starring the amazing Chadwick Boseman, may he rest in peace, as Prince T'Challa. Just as Simba had to overthrow the inept leadership of his uncle Scar to take his rightful position as king, Prince T'Challa had to overthrow Killmonger to take back his rightful position as king of Wakanda.

If two of the biggest movie franchises in the world have this as a central theme, it's worth exploring.

All around the world, the lion is considered to be the king of the jungle. (Again, for the purposes of this teaching, the terms *lion* and *king* are gender neutral.) However, the lion has a lot of reasons to doubt its kingship, because there are many other animals in the animal kingdom that have qualities that outperform the lion's. For example:

- The lion is not the smartest animal in the jungle. The monkey is smarter.
- The lion is not the fastest animal in the jungle. The cheetah is faster.
- The lion is not the biggest animal in the jungle. The elephant is bigger.
- The lion is not the heaviest animal in the jungle. The hippo is heavier.
- The lion is not the tallest animal in the jungle. The giraffe is taller.
- The lion is not the most agile animal in the jungle. The snake is more agile.
- The lion is not the most populous animal in the jungle. The ant is more populous.

What's my point? It's very simple. Let me translate this into terms you can relate to.

- The lion may not have the biggest social media following.
- The lion may not have the perfect relationship history.
- The lion may not have the biggest Facebook ad budget.
- The lion may not have graduated top of its class with honors.
- The lion may not have been raised with both parents in the home.
- The lion may not have been dealt the perfect deck of cards to be "successful."

- The lion may not have the perfect pedigree to climb the corporate ladder quickly.
- The lion may not have gotten all the funding needed to start its business the right way.
- The lion may not have discovered its purpose and passion until later in life.

But . . . in spite of all of these "disadvantages," the lion is still the king of the jungle. For one powerful reason: the lion believes that it is. The lion looks at all of those other animals (with different qualifications) as breakfast, lunch, dinner, or a snack for its pride. It sees all those other animals as edible.

And so must you! I'm not saying you have to eat meat (for all you vegetarians out there); what I am saying is that you must sit on the motorcycle of life the right way, so that you can take your rightful position as the king of your own interpersonal and professional Pride Rock. It's your birthright to be on top. To be the best!

Da Cat Don't Care

About two years ago, I was talking to my older brother, Mike, at a restaurant. During that time in his life, he was down on his luck and not really in the most ideal place professionally. After listening to him complain for a few minutes (and I would have been complaining too, had that been my story), I used a "pattern interrupt" to shift his state by asking him a question he was not expecting.

I said, "Mike, do you know why they say that you should never feed a stray cat?" He was like "What? What are you talking about? Yes, I know exactly why they say you should never feed a stray cat, but what in the world does that have to do with where I am in my career, and my business not being where I want it to be?"

I continued, "Mike, just trust me and answer the question. Why do they say that you should never feed a stray cat?" He sucked his teeth a little, smiled at me, and said, "Man, because once you feed it, it will keep coming back!"

I said, "YES . . . Yes, it will. Now, Mike, let me ask you a more powerful question. When the cat comes back, does the cat care what kind of car you drive? Does the cat care how many Italian suits are in your closet? Does the cat evaluate your retirement portfolio? Does the cat ask you for six months of bank statements? Does the cat care whether you live in the 'good part of town' before it partakes of the food or drink that you provide?" And Mike chuckled and said, "No," and I responded, "Exactly, Mike, because the truth is, *da cat don't care*. It just wants to be fed! It just wants something good to eat. And as long as you give it some food, it will keep coming back."

My point is that my brother, at that moment, was dealing with impostor syndrome, something that almost all high achievers experience at some point in their success journey. He felt that his lack of all the perfect credentials at that time was disqualifying him from the success he wanted in his business.

I am pleased to report that Mike is killing it now in the insurance and financial services industry, because he has taken his rightful position.

Please hear me. Every single day, there are millions of people all around the world who are looking for the solutions that you provide. However, you can only provide those solutions once you get over your own perceived limitations and begin to reposition yourself. Stop looking at the past and looking at all the mistakes that you feel disqualify you. Turn around and sit on the bike of life the right way and take your rightful position, all the while keeping in mind that *da cat don't care* about the things that you feel are your limitations. The cat just wants good food! And if you feed it good food in the form of autographing your work with excellence, you will quickly realize that the cat will keep coming back.

In other words, both cats don't care—the small stray cat that you feed doesn't care about your limitations, and the big cat in the jungle doesn't care about its limitations because he sees all those "more qualified" animals as a meal.

So right now, I want you to list seven things that until now you've thought of as "disqualifications" about yourself that you know have been holding you back from the personal and professional success you desire.

1. _____

2. _____

3. _____

4. _____

5. _____

6. _____

7. _____

Thank you for your honesty. That's so powerful, real, and transparent. Now let's do two things with this list. First, next to each of the statements, write this one phrase: "Da Cat Don't Care!" Second, go back over each one of those seven things you listed and, in your journal, write down a more powerful way to reframe that reality about yourself. (You learned how to do this in chapter 5.) Remember, facts and truth are two different things.

Take your rightful position. Now is your time!

Five Ways You Can Shift Higher and Tune Up the Motorcycle of Your Life

1. To live life to the fullest, you've got to sit on the motorcycle of life the right way and not think that the best part of your life is in the past. The rest of your life is truly the best of your life. Embrace that. Change your position so that you can change your condition.

2. The front wheel of your bike is your free-spinning wheel of vision. It's for steering and direction. Always keep a vision for your future ahead of you; don't limit or restrict it. The back wheel is fatter and thicker because that's your past, but it's also where your power comes from. Use the throttle to leverage the lessons from your past to propel you forward powerfully.

3. The left brake controls the back wheel—your past. The right brake controls the front wheel—your future. When you're deep in the

curves of life, never jam the front brake; instead, drag the back brake. In the middle of the challenges of your life, know how much to use which brakes to keep you moving forward.

4. Lean into the curves of life and business by asking powerful questions whose answers can give you the fuel you need to roll the throttle, because when you're deep in a curve, acceleration is the only thing that pulls you back out. Take massive action on your goals and dreams—in the middle of your personal and pro- fessional crisis—and watch those curves disappear as quickly as they show up.

5. Always remember that *da cat don't care*. What you think is your dis- advantage or disqualifying aspect could be the very thing that's your greatest strength. Take your rightful position as the king of your own personal and professional Pride Rock.

Shift to Defensive Driving to Avoid the Four Potholes You'll Encounter along Your Journey

Most of the time, hitting a pothole in a car or truck can feel like a speed bump and does little to no real damage to your overall journey. However, hitting the same pothole on a motorcycle can cause you to crash and ruin your bike; it can even cause a fatal accident, depending on how fast you're going upon impact with the pothole. Four main variables are what make potholes so dangerous:

1. They sneak up on you without warning or prior notice.
2. On first glance, you can't determine how deep they are.
3. Sometimes you can't tell how wide the hole is or how jagged the edges are.
4. You often don't know the full extent of the damage they will cause until after you've already rolled through one.

What's my point?

You must drive very defensively on your motorcycle to avoid the potholes that inevitably show up in life and business to derail your success. Over the course of my life, I've encountered many potholes. I'm sure that by looking at the cover of this book and reading my bio you may think that I've always been "successful" and can't relate to potholes, but trust me, I've had many things attempt to derail my success.

- As a child, I was labeled an "at-risk" youth and told I wouldn't amount to much.
- As a preteen, my stepfather was extremely abusive, and I wanted to run away.
- As a teenager, I was inches away from a heinous hate crime that rocked our city.
- Also as a teenager, I witnessed my mother experience domestic violence.
- My twenty-year journey as an entrepreneur has been rattled with challenges.
- As an adult, I've experienced failure with a real estate business and a clothing line.
- As an adult, I've experienced the pain of divorce, having to heal from the brokenness it caused.

All of these things rocked my self-confidence, self-esteem, and self-worth and how I saw myself and the world. These were all different potholes along my journey. Some were just on the road, and some I actually created on my own along the way. Have you ever created the very potholes that have derailed your own success? We call this self-sabotage.

Take a moment and make a list in your journal of a few things that have happened in your life or career that have tried to derail your success. And know that even though our lists may look radically different, that's not really what matters. Pain is pain. Failure is failure. Hardship is hardship. What matters is not the specifics of what we go through but how we shift so that we can enjoy the journey of life and business successfully.

While doing the research for this chapter, I visited several biking blogs recounting the stories of the massive accidents that occurred when motorcyclists thought they were skilled enough to just "ride over" potholes, and of the horrific damage that both their bikes and their bodies experienced. Overall, the best advice from everyone in the biking community is to avoid potholes at all costs. Period. This takes maneuvering and constantly being on the lookout to ensure that the path that you're riding down is one that is smooth and pothole-free.

I've been working with high achievers globally for the last twenty years through my live and virtual experiential keynote presentations and also through my annual conference, the Full Throttle Experience. From what I've learned along the way, I've determined that although there are many different types of potholes you can encounter along your journey, there are four types that high achievers specifically encounter; if they do not avoid them, these potholes can cause rim damage, blown tires, broken front and rear suspension, and ultimately a flying-over-the-handlebars accident that could ruin them personally or professionally.

As I mentioned earlier, potholes don't give you much advance notice; they just show up on the road. You don't have adequate time to react, and that's why you must be constantly looking ahead—not just at the drivers in front of you but also at the road conditions. Each of these four potholes can just sneak up on you if you're not careful. Keep your eyes focused forward every day and drive defensively on the motorcycle of life to avoid them.

The Pothole of Burnout

Are you feeling burned out? Be honest with yourself.

There's no one else around, so you can be honest with me.

I want to take some extra time on this one, because it's a huge global issue.

According to a recent article in *HR Exchange*, burnout cases have increased to the point where the World Health Organization (WHO) has officially recognized burnout as an occupational phenomenon.[1] In fact, WHO has included it in its eleventh revision of the International Classification of Diseases. The handbook describes burnout as "a syndrome conceptualized as resulting from chronic workplace stress that has not been successfully managed."

In addition, Gallup recently surveyed more than seventy-five hundred full-time employees about burnout. Of those workers, 23% said they felt burned out more often than not. An additional 44% reported feeling burned out sometimes.[2] In other words, nearly two-thirds of full-time workers are dealing with burnout at some point while at work.

Here are a few ways to know that you're approaching or running into the pothole of burnout.

- Are you constantly irritable, hypercritical, negative, and jaded in your perspective?
- Do you find it hard most days to concentrate on getting a task done?
- Do you achieve things and feel lackluster about your accomplishment?
- Do you constantly use food, alcohol, drugs, or other means to self-medicate?
- Do you feel exhausted no matter how much sleep you get?

You could be at burnout. And this affects parents, entrepreneurs, and people from every professional industry, not only traditional nine-to-five employees.

Maneuver around the pothole of burnout when it shows up by trying the following:

- Practice regular self-care.
- Cut your workday off at a certain time each day, and unplug afterward.
- Don't check work-related emails and texts after hours.
- Take quarterly staycations, weekend trips, or small getaways to recharge.
- Get good rest each night—at least seven to eight hours.
- Spend the first and last hour of each day away from technology.

The Pothole of Loneliness and Isolation

Everyone talks about climbing the ladder of success, but very few people talk about the loneliness and isolation that often accompany that journey. Let me ask you a hard question: Do you struggle with feeling lonely or isolated sometimes?

According to an article in *Occupational Health & Safety*, more than 60% of Americans report feeling lonely, left out, poorly understood, and lacking companionship, according to a recent report by Cigna Insurance.[3] Male and younger workers bear the heaviest burden—and workplace culture may be a major contributing factor.

I'll be very transparent with you and share that at many times in my life, I've felt lonely and somewhat isolated. Most recently, I moved back to the Tampa Bay area after living in Dallas/Fort Worth for a few years. I relocated to a nice suburb in Tampa called Wesley Chapel. However, the majority of my friends and the "happenings" in town were about forty minutes away from where I lived. So, for the first two years that I was back in town, I felt lonely. I was very successful and very accomplished and in demand, but when I would come home, I always felt lonely. I lived in a great, safe subdivision, but I was one of the only single people I knew in my neighborhood. Everywhere I looked, all I saw were couples and families. I was a single dad and a busy entrepreneur who traveled a lot. (Footnote—traveling a lot can be very lonely also.)

We all are hardwired for connection and relationships. No matter how much we accomplish, achieve, and manifest—things and status can only get you so far. Friends, companionship, fellowship, and connections are essential for living life to the fullest.

Maneuver around the pothole of loneliness when it shows up by trying the following:

- Use MeetUp.com to find special-interest groups that do things you already enjoy.
- Use your NextDoor app to connect with people in and around your neighborhood.
- Use Facebook or LinkedIn to find networking meetings happening around you.
- Let your friends and family know when you have free nights and weekends.
- Let people in. When people ask how you're doing, be honest. Stop covering up. If you want some company, companionship, or just people around you . . . say so!

The Pothole of Overwhelm

No statistics needed for this one! Here's the cold, hard truth. Most high achievers struggle with overwhelm for one primary reason: we consider the word *help* a curse word. Yep, most of us don't like to ask for help. We try to do it all ourselves. Have you ever been guilty of this? Many of us graduated from the University of I Can Do It All Myself. Overwhelm is a major pothole because when you try to do everything yourself, you rarely do a great job at the task because you're so stressed and anxious about it that the negative energy of the pressure to perform bleeds over into the quality of the work.

We tend to become overwhelmed when we think about too many aspects of a project all at the same time; or too many components of a process at the same time; or too many elements of a problem, situation, or dilemma all at the same time—without the adequate mental, emotional, financial, logistical, or tactical resources at our disposal to effectively resolve the issue(s). Compounded with this is the pride that most high achievers carry; we don't like to look, feel, or come across as weak or unable, so we do a poor job of delegating.

Delegating is one of the keys to maneuvering around the pothole of overwhelm. You can't get better daily if you're constantly overwhelmed, and you certainly can't live life to the fullest that way.

A recent study out of the UK suggests that as much as 74% of professionals feel so stressed that they feel overwhelmed and unable to cope.[4]

Maneuver around the pothole of overwhelm when it shows up by trying the following:

- Let go of your ego's need for control and allow others to assist you.
- Exercise transparency and vulnerability by allowing others in emotionally, so that they can understand the weight you carry.
- Break up all your big projects, assignments, and tasks into bite-size chunks.
- Take small, consistent daily action on tasks that move you closer to your goals.
- Reward yourself more for the actions and steps you're already taking.

The Pothole of Rejection

By now you should be ready for me to stop listing potholes, because I know that on some level you can probably relate to most or all of these. Here's the last one—the fear of rejection or just rejection itself. No one likes to get rejected. It's not fun. No matter how it shows up, none of us actually enjoy the process of not getting chosen, selected, approved, accepted, validated, affirmed, and/or deemed "worthy." And rejection can show up in every area of our lives.

- Your kids growing up and not wanting to hang with you as much
- Someone on a dating app not swiping right and matching with you
- Getting passed over for an important promotion at work
- Auditioning for a role, part, or opportunity and not being chosen
- Trying out for a sports team, band, dance group, or talent team and not making the cut
- People not signing up for your programs or services after an educational webinar
- Your significant other not wanting intimacy with you on a particular night
- Members of your family not inviting you to a family gathering
- Your spouse deciding they want to file for divorce
- Being turned down for the mortgage to buy your dream home this year
- Not getting approved for a major credit card or line of credit you need
- Approaching a perfect stranger who you think is attractive, and they dismiss you
- Entering a scholarship contest to win money for tuition and you don't get chosen

Rejection shows up in a million ways in our daily lives all the time. We all experience it. Even the people who you think life always says yes to—trust me, somewhere along their journey, they have experienced massive rejection.

The pothole of rejection can be a very dangerous one because too much rejection can totally wreck your self-esteem, self-worth, and self-confidence. It can make you feel that you're not good enough. Have you ever felt like that? I know 500% that I have.

Although I've had a ton of successes in life, I've dealt with a massive amount of rejection in my life also:

- Not getting into the fraternity I wanted in college
- Getting fired from a corporate job
- Being rejected for high-fee speaking engagements
- Agents rejecting book proposals
- My reality TV show not being selected by TV execs at a pitch conference
- Experiencing divorce from someone whom I cared for very much
- Feeling as though my speaking ability is viewed as a threat in many circles

One of the greatest lessons I've learned about rejection can be summed up in this statement:

Rejection is hidden selection.

What I've learned is that when life deselects me for something that I *think* I wanted, it is just God's way of selecting me for what I really *want* and *need* that is for my greatest and highest good. When you're not chosen for something or someone, consider it life's way of helping you dodge a bullet and instead prepare something even better for you. Think about some of the many famous people who made it big after massive rejection.

- *Chicken Soup for the Soul* got rejected by 144 publishers before it was picked up, and now it's one of the best-selling franchises in human history.[5]
- J. K. Rowling was rejected by twelve publishers before *Harry Potter* got picked up.[6]

- Steven Spielberg was rejected by the USC School of Theatre, Film and Television three times.[7]

- Walt Disney was fired from a local newspaper for a "lack of creativity, imagination and good ideas."[8]

- Vincent van Gogh's paintings were rejected throughout his lifetime; he sold only two pieces while he was alive.[9]

- Oprah was fired from a local TV station as a reporter because the management said she "wasn't fit for television."[10]

As you can see, if you've been rejected, you're in great company. Obviously, the pothole of rejection is inevitable; how you navigate around it is what matters. Maneuver around the pothole of rejection when it shows up by trying the following:

- Separate the event/rejection from you as a person (easier said than done).

- Don't give up or quit; keep trying and keep going after that which you desire.

- Every time you hear "no," just think "next" and keep moving forward.

- Find the silver lining in the situation by looking for areas for growth.

- If the rejection is severe, consider seeing a mental health professional for therapy.

These are just four of the many different types of potholes that can cause massive damage to the motorcycle ride of your life and business. To learn about others, visit the Free Book Bonuses section of www.ShiftIntoAHigher Gear.com. To succeed on your journey, drive to enjoy the scenery and drive to arrive, but also drive defensively by not only looking for the vehicles in front of and beside you but also inspecting the road conditions and leaning left and right as needed to avoid hitting the various potholes you will encounter. And listen: none of us are perfect. If you do hit a pothole, pull over immediately, inspect your bike for any possible damage, and keep on riding, but be careful and diligent, because what you cannot avoid you must be prepared for. And unlike a car, most motorcycles don't come with a spare tire. If you get a flat tire, you'll need to call roadside assistance. I've been riding for ten years, and thank God, I've never hit a pothole on my motorcycle, but I've hit plenty of them in life and business. And that's exactly why chapter 12 is so important.

Five Ways You Can Shift Higher and Tune Up the Motorcycle of Your Life

1. The question is never whether you'll encounter a pothole but how you will maneuver to avoid them. Unfavorable road conditions are inevitable. It's how you handle them that really matters. No matter how strong, tough, and skilled you are, it's always better to avoid potholes rather than riding through them.

2. The pothole of burnout is very real. Make a decision right now that you deserve some time off. Here's a thought: use some of your PTO if you have it. If your career isn't set up that way, create time for yourself to recharge. Every device that you use daily requires time to be recharged—and so do you!

3. Sometimes you struggle with loneliness because you've trained people to believe that you're always too busy. We are hard-wired for human connection and relationship. Reduce your screen time, be safe, get out there, and connect with people so that you can avoid the pothole of isolation and loneliness.

4. How do you eat an elephant? One bite at a time! The best way to avoid overwhelm is to take every big thing in your life and break it down into small, daily baby steps. Also, find people to help you accomplish your goals as a team, because success is better together.

5. Remember that rejection is hidden selection. What one person hates, someone else loves. One person's floor is another person's ceiling.

What one group of people discards, another group of people will esteem and honor. Rejection is simply life's way of helping you dodge bullets and position you for the best opportunities to come your way with grace and ease.

CHAPTER 12

Shift from Simple Goal Setting to Transformational Goal Getting

---

I . . . am . . . so . . . proud . . . of . . . you!

You've made it to the final chapter of this book, and I can't tell you how incredibly proud of you I am and how honored I am to have spent this time with you. But we are not done yet. There are still a few key principles that I need to download into your heart, mind, and spirit to assist you as you shift into a higher gear.

To put bookends on this concept of living life to the fullest, we must talk about why we are doing all this shifting to begin with. What's the point of making all these big and small changes in the way we think and live? We hope that the purpose is to help us actually achieve our wildest and most impassioned goals and dreams . . . right?

My dear friend, I want you to shift from mere goal *setting*, which anyone can do, to actual goal *getting*! I want you to successfully make the transition from

- Wanting to walking
- Dreaming to doing
- Pontification to participation
- Information to implementation

- Thinking to trying
- Intention to immersion
- Inspiration to manifestation

If three birds are sitting on a branch and
one decides to fly away, how many are left?
All three, because the one just decided.
Decision is not enough. We must take ACTION!

—Author unknown

Wanting is not enough. Dreaming is not enough. Planning is not enough. These are part of achieving a goal, but they're not enough. We must take action. Anyone can set a goal, but it takes a champion to reach a goal. We must roll the throttle!

I want you to bring into material form all that you conceptualize in your mind and heart as possible for yourself. I want you to become a manifester. To become a manifester of your goals and dreams, you have to change, because who you've been will not get you where you want to be. That process requires change. Throughout this book, I have been nudging you toward making small shifts that equal big changes in your life and profession. Now let's cement that with a final challenge to change so that I can help you achieve your highest goals at a more accelerated rate.

Goals Defined

I define a goal simply as a predetermined success point; a place of arrival thought of in advance. Basically, a goal is premeditated achievement. A goal is what you decide today about where you want to be tomorrow, and taking steps today to make sure that happens.

The best way to predict the future is to create it.

—Attributed to Peter Drucker

- Imagine the game of football with no end zones.

- Imagine the game of basketball with no hoops.
- Imagine the game of baseball with no home plate.

That's how crazy your life looks without clearly defined goals.

When I speak to corporations, associations, pro sports teams, nonprofit groups, direct selling organizations, and ministries globally, I talk about how all goal setting can be broken down into ten simple categories. I'm going to go out on a limb and suggest to you that anything that you want to accomplish or achieve can be grouped under one of these ten areas of life.

1. Interpersonal, mental, and emotional—mindset, mental health, and emotional mastery

2. Professional and career—job, business growth, work or livelihood, promotions

3. Spiritual and faith—expressions of your God consciousness and beliefs

4. Family and household—biological, blended, or a combination; kids, siblings, kinfolk

5. Health and wellness—nutrition, exercise, medical appointments, supplements, routine

6. Financial and money—wealth building, budgeting, planning, investing, retirement

7. Philanthropy and service—giving, serving, volunteering, and contributing

8. Social activity and community—friends, outings, social media, neighbors, gatherings

9. Love and relationships—romantic interests, dating, marriage, life partnerships

10. Leisure and hobbies—special interests, side passions, side hustles, vacations

My challenge to you is to set one hundred goals for yourself. It's much easier than you think, because one hundred goals are really only ten goals in each area.

Maybe your health and wellness goals could look something like this:

Health and Wellness Goals for [Your Name Here]

1. Drink 64 oz. of water daily.
2. Spend twenty minutes each day in the sunshine.
3. Maintain my ideal weight of ____ lbs without diet fads or gimmicks.
4. Exercise for at least thirty minutes Monday through Friday.
5. Plan my meals in advance so that I eat nutritiously six days per week.
6. Enjoy a cheat day one day per week.
7. Lift heavy weights two times per week and do cardio three times per week.
8. Take a gender-specific liquid multivitamin each day.
9. Keep up with my dental, vision, primary care, and specialist doctor visits.
10. Play my favorite sport or outdoor activity as often as possible with friends.

Keep in mind that this list of possible goals is a very vanilla list. Feel free to make yours much more robust than this or milder than this. But one thing I want this list to model is the specificity. Create lists like this for all the other nine areas of your life and wow—you will be well on your way to shifting from being merely a goal setter to a manifesting goal getter!

The Eight R's to Manifest Any Goal

Whatever goals you want to achieve, use these eight principles (the eight R's) to get them, and you will have them. This isn't something I read in some book; this is what I've lived and know to be true. In fact, I want you to think of a huge goal, a goal that if you could achieve it, would make having read this book 500% worth it. Write that goal down and put it in your journal.

Now, with that goal in mind, let's compile the following to assist you.

1. Room

This is where most people go way wrong. Coming out the gate of the journey toward their goals, they hit the pothole of overwhelm because they've never made room for the goals and dreams they desire. My friend, before you go adding anything new on the proverbial plate of your life, you need to decide what needs to come off that plate first. If you're a high achiever, which you are, your plate is already full of stuff. So the question is, what stuff needs to come off your plate, what skin do you need to shed so you can make room for something new? Whom do you need to let go of so that you can attract the person you really deserve? What clothes in your closet do you need to give away, sell, or donate to make room for that new wardrobe you want? Isn't it time to clean your garage of all that old stuff you don't even need so that you'll have space for a recreational vehicle or, perhaps . . . a new motorcycle? Your goals and dreams are like embryos; they need space to grow. So make a list in your journal and number it 1 through 10. Name ten things, people, mindsets, attitudes, or habits that you need to get rid of, which will make room for the goals that you actually want to achieve. You can't even start your journey if you haven't first made room!

2. Reasons

Most people go wrong with their goal achievement because they focus too much on the "what" of the goal instead of the "why." Why do you want to achieve the goals you have in mind? Why is more important than what! The why is what's going to keep you motivated and inspired when the way seems long, hard, and mostly uphill. You must have compelling reasons why you want what you want. As Simon Sinek would say, "Start with Why!" For every goal you write down in your journal, give yourself three reasons why you must achieve it.

3. Resources

Once you know why you want what you want, you need to go on a scavenger hunt to gather, rally, and assemble all the resources that you currently have at your disposal to help you pull off this goal. What do you already have in your possession that will help you achieve your dreams faster? When I wanted to produce my own reality TV show, I already lived in a city that had mansions for rent, and one of my best friends was a TV producer, so I had a location and a creative brain and partner at my disposal. You will gain tremendous momentum toward your goals once you realize that you have more wood for the fire than you realize. Make a list of all the existing resources you already have. Yes, you probably need more stuff, but start with what you have!

One of the best resources I can recommend is pictures of the goals you seek in their achieved state. If you want a new car, go sit in the one you want (even if you don't qualify for it financially at this time) and put that photo on your wall as a resource and a source of inspiration for you. Notice how the entries in every successful cookbook have three main components: a list of ingredients, a description of the process of mixing the ingredients and cooking the actual dish, and (usually) a photo of the completed master-piece. The authors of these books fully understand that in order to replicate any master dish, you certainly need resources. You also need the next R.

4. Road Map

You need a plan. You need a strategy. You need a route to take. And I wish that plotting out the fastest route to achieve your goals was as easy as pulling up Waze or Google Maps, but it isn't. However, one of the best ways to draw a road map for actually getting the goals you set is by looking at prior models of success that already exist. In other words, look at people who have succeeded at doing what you want to do. What was their process? What was their path? How did they go about pulling it off? You want to learn from and glean from people who have actually done what you want to do. When I'm pulling off a big event, I never talk to people who have not hosted big events before; as well meaning as they can be, they can't really help me. I connect only with people whose information can influence my road map. The best way to create a road map for your goal is to study those who have arrived at a destination similar to the one you seek.

5. Rewards

On the journey to success in anything that you want, you need milestones along the way that incentivize you to keep going. The human mind loves rewards. Your brain loves releasing dopamine and serotonin—two very powerful chemicals that make you feel great, happy, successful, meaningful, and alive. So as you take action on your goals and dreams, make sure that you reward yourself in small ways all along the journey. A reward can be a small snack or a massage or a weekend trip that you plan for yourself and someone you care about. It can be watching a favorite show or taking a long bath or ordering from a favorite restaurant or treating your family and friends to a night on the town, but whatever you choose, do something weekly to reward yourself as you strive to achieve your goals. Your brain will inspire you to go far beyond goal setting and shift into goal getting.

6. Relationships

This simple principle is like pouring gasoline on the fire of your goals. It takes only one person to like you, recommend you, or refer you to take your goals from a possibility to a reality. The right relationships will help you achieve your goals in record time and at lightning speed. As we discussed in chapter 8, who you ride with really and truly does matter. Ask yourself this simple question: "Who needs to know that I am trying to achieve this goal?" Then ask yourself, "Who knows someone who needs to know that I am trying to achieve this goal?" Make a list of your existing connections—you are much closer to your next open door than you realize.

7. Resolve

Once you set your mind and heart on the goal that you must manifest, you will need a healthy and unwavering dose of resolve to see it through to manifestation. In other words, you've gotta keep your hands on the throttle. You can't quit, and you can't give up. You must be determined to see it through. Here's a cold, hard truth: you will experience failure on the way to your biggest goals. You will. You will fail on the way to something big, and you will fail on the way to something small. So you might as well go for the big! Make up in your mind before you even start the journey that you will not quit. When things get hard, you will dig in, you will take breaks as you need to, but you will continue to fight until your goals are realized. Another way to experience resolve is to express gratitude as if you already have the very thing you want. Start to journal and to declare out of your mouth expressions of thanksgiving as if you already possess the things that you want, and that declaration of resolve will speed up your goal-getting process.

8. Real Experience

If you want to train for a fitness competition, actually go to one; you will be more motivated than ever to actually make it happen. If you want to learn yoga, go on an instructor retreat and watch how much passion you develop for it. If you want to become a speaker as I did, attend the National Speakers Association annual convention and be immersed in the experience of meeting hundreds of people who do this for a living. My point? Find a real experience that puts you knee-deep in the thing that you want to do and puts you around the people who have done it, are doing it, want to do it. What you learn, who you will meet, and what you will discover about yourself will astound you.

Let me ask you a powerful question. Go back to your journal where you wrote down that big goal you want to achieve. Now ask yourself which of the eight R's you still need. Apply these eight R's to your big goals and dreams and watch yourself radically shift from goal setting to powerful, manifesting goal getting.

Five Ways You Can Shift Higher and Tune Up the Motorcycle of Your Life

1. The idea in life is to be a goal getter, not just a goal setter. Be willing to make the necessary transitions in order to experience success.
2. Defining your goals has four pivotal steps. First, you must see your goal mentally before anything else. Once you see your goal in

your mind, writing it down brings it to life. From there, creating a visual to go with it then helps you create the experience to match it. These steps show that achieving your goals takes work but that they all start with a simple thought.

3. Manifestation is what we all want. But we have to ensure that we're walking the right steps so that it can occur, without fail and without delay. The eight R's—room, reasons, resources, road maps, rewards, relationships, resolve, and real experience—will enable you to manifest on a consistent basis.

4. You have to get sick and tired of being sick and tired. When you become comfortable with the pity party, you've entered a dangerous place. Shift off of the nail of compromise and roll the throttle by taking consistent imperfect action.

5. Shifting into a higher gear takes place when you finish what you've started. If you want to always go higher, be consistent with crossing the finish line each time you start something. Goal setting involves starting; goal getting is all about finishing!

CONCLUSION

I'll See You on the Open Road

The word *commencement*, which we are accustomed to hearing at graduations, does not really mean the end of something but rather the beginning of a new journey. You are about to embark on a brand-new life, one where you get to shift into a higher gear in every area of your life that you select.

My goal has been to distill for you the steps I've taken and the steps taken by extremely successful people whom I know and study, so that you can top yourself consistently and live the ultimate life that you desire. I've given you a lot of tools, ideas, concepts, research, and action steps, but at the end of the day, it's very easy to read a book and not implement what it teaches. I've been guilty of that in the past myself. I think we all have been. But this is not that type of book, and you're no longer that type of person.

Regardless of whether you ride a motorcycle regularly, used to ride years ago, don't ride but have always wanted to, or had zero interest in riding before this book, I know that you now see some powerful and profound parallels between motorcycle riding and aspects of your life and career that you want to take to the next level. Yes, I've been using the motorcycle simply as a metaphor; however, adding this incredible hobby, pastime, and/ or mode of transportation to your life could be a game changer for you as it was for me. Whether you take lessons, rent a motorcycle on your next vacation, or decide to own one, I challenge you to bring all these lessons to life through the experience of actually riding a motorcycle. Trust me, done safely it's one of the coolest experiences of life.

My single request of you is that you allow the action you take as a result of this book to make you change. Let this be the context, let this be the moment, and let this be the time that you actuate all that you've experienced in this book.

My final challenge to you is a call to action. When you started this book, I asked you, "When you hear the phrase *shift into a higher gear*, what comes to mind?" Now that you've experienced the content of this book, I ask you that same question again.

_____

_____

_____

Now compare what you felt this phrase meant at the beginning of this book to how you feel and how you responded now.

Big difference, isn't there? That's a great thing. We've unpacked so much amazing material in this book.

Key Lessons from Each Chapter

Let's do a quick yet necessary recap of the key lessons from each chapter, because I want to make sure that you got everything I offered in this book.

Get 1% Better Daily

It's my sincere hope and prayer that from chapter 1 you gleaned a powerful understanding that it's in the small, incremental shifts that big change and transformation take place. You're already doing great things, or you would not have made it this far in a book like this, so I applaud you. Now simply take all you've done and shift it into a higher gear. Remember that riding is a journey, not solely a destination. Enjoy the ride, because there is no there . . . *there*. Keep in mind that your best is behind you, so you must use your present to get 1% better each and every day.

The Movie of Your Life Is Meant to Be Experienced in 3-D

I hope that chapter 2 really rocked your world and is still bothering you in a really good way. I pray that from this landmark chapter, you've adopted a totally new mindset about learning to live 3-D. And although most of us were never taught to live three-dimensionally, I hope that now you understand the power of living wide, long, and deep. Some of the most remarkable people in human history didn't live that long, but they changed the world because they lived their years to the fullest. From now on, my friend, promise me that you'll invest in living the width of your years and the depth of your years, while you celebrate the length of your years. Celebrate the width and depth along the way as well.

Either Change or Be Changed by Change

What I enjoyed unpacking for you in chapter 3 was the importance of acceptance. Always remember that when you ride the motorcycle of life, you have to accept the elements as they are, but as a great leader committed to change, you also get to see things better than they are and ultimately make things the way you see them. Any change worth pursuing is going to make you walk through all six phases of the change process: It must change, I must change it, I can change it, I will change it, I am changing it, and I have changed it!

Celebration is also a very important part of making it through your change process. Get through each phase with a grateful and inspired attitude and you'll not just change but transform.

Lean into It and Put Your Wait into Your Future

Chapter 4 was a challenge to get you out of Just Enough land and focus on really going in on the things you want in order to create success in life. We talked about putting both your weight and your wait into the things that matter most to you. We also talked about the keys to cultivating excellence and how excellence must be your new standard if you want to successfully shift into that higher gear. Remember to be like a stamp and stick to one thing until it delivers.

Kick Back Your Kickstand and Focus on Truth vs. Facts

The moment you use an excuse, you engage the kickstand and stall the ride of your life. Yep. The motorcycle of your life can't and won't function as long as the kickstand is down. Every excuse that you give yourself is another kickstand that supports your bike, but just know that you're also not going anywhere. Remember to use the power of cognitive reframing to turn old excuses into powerful and purposeful declarations. And no matter how expensive your house, car, clothes, or that next vacation—nothing is more expensive than your excuses! Don't rely on excuses. Ride the bike properly and rely on yourself.

Faith Your Fears to Death

If you've never watched *The Karate Kid, Part III*, make sure you watch it. Great movie! In chapter 6, I really pushed you to get honest about the role that fear could be playing in your journey toward success. Remember that you have only two choices in life: to live your dreams or live your fears. It's really that simple. And although you probably listed a lot of fears that you may now be wrestling with, as we all are, there are only two that you were biologically blessed with. Outside of those two fears, all else is learned behavior, and you can learn faith just as quickly as you can learn fear. Also remember that fear is only doing its job. So feel the fear, appreciate the message it's trying to send you, and take action anyway, because that's the definition of courage.

Change Your Emotional Home Address

Everything changed for me when I learned that anything in my life that I said I wanted could be boiled down to an emotion. The engine of the motorcycle of your life is indeed the quality of your emotions. The quality of your emotions is at the center, the very core, of who you are as a person. Remember that you will always find your way back to your emotional home. Whatever emotions you want to experience on a daily basis, make a decision not just to want to feel the emotion as if it's in some faraway place but to actually embody the emotion. Be honest with yourself as to the emotions that until now have run the show in your life, and make an intentional choice today that you will now live at a new emotional home. You have a new address, and gratitude lives there with you each and every day.

Pick Your Posse on Purpose

I hope that one of the greatest messages you gleaned from chapter 8 was the importance of the relationships and connections in your life, because who you ride with is vital. What did you learn from your posse audit? Regardless of the results, I'm hoping that it helped you realize that we must be intentional about all the relationships in our lives, especially if these folks are going to ride with us on the journey.

Do you already have mentors, mates, and mentees in your life? Is it time to shift those connections to the next level? At this season of your life, what accountability partners and masterminds do you need in order to better your best?

Remember that it's ultimately your relationship with yourself that is most important. You will always ride with yourself. You can't *not* ride with yourself, so always work harder on yourself than you do on anything else, and you'll be successful.

Your Life Should Know Only Forward

Chapter 9 is one of my favorites because it really focuses on developing a deep desire to always move forward in life. Regardless of what happens in your life, no matter what goes wrong, no matter who leaves, no matter what opportunities you get, no matter what doors don't open—my friend, understand that you were built to go forward only! You were meant to live your life in Drive. Motorcycles are built primarily with one gear, and that's Drive. By staying in Drive, you get to avoid the other, less productive gears—Park, Reverse, and Neutral—that often come along depending on the various circumstances in life. No matter which gear you may find yourself in, you can always shift higher by applying the various cure strategies that I outlined in this chapter.

Take Your Rightful Position

If by reading this book you've realized that you've been playing too small, then congratulations. That's a fantastic thing to understand, because you can't change your condition until you change your position. It's time to take your rightful position. The days of you sitting on the motorcycle of your life backward and living as if the best of your life has already happened are over! And whether it's *The Lion King* or *Black Panther*, the message is still the same: you belong on top. You belong in control of your destiny. The best way to take back control is by realizing that *da cat don't care*. Regardless of your own limiting beliefs about yourself (which we all have), you were born to be amazing. So stop focusing on the failures and successes of yesterday, yester-week, yester-month, and yesteryear; shift higher by taking your rightful position. Return to your throne.

There's No Spare on a Motorcycle, So Avoid Blowing Out Your Tire

Because we live in such a fast-moving world, we often take potholes for granted. In cars, we just run right over them without a second thought. However, because we are living the bike way, potholes can be deadly, so we must avoid them at all costs. Being a defensive driver has never been more important than it is when your goal is to shift into a higher gear. Will you be able to avoid all potholes? Absolutely not. However, there are four types that can do some major damage; you'll want to practice swerving as much as you can so that when potholes arrive, you won't be as affected. As high achievers, we can easily fall prey to the potholes of burnout, isolation, overwhelm, and rejection that keep us from enjoying the ride of life. Maneuvering is the key. Enjoy the ride, but stay on the lookout for potholes and prepare for them in advance by making sure you keep your eyes on the road.

A Goal Always Works Harder on You Than You Do on the Goal

It's my sincere hope and prayer that from chapter 12 you gleaned clarity around the key difference between goal setting and actual manifestation through goal getting. I hope to have inspired you to reach higher by setting higher standards for yourself and those you influence. Remember, a goal is simply a predetermined success point. If I could speak with you privately,

I'm sure that anything you would tell me that you want could easily fit into one of the ten categories of goals that I listed in this chapter. But it's not enough just to have a goal; you need to break the goal down into the smaller actionable steps that you can take on a daily basis to manifest it. Whatever you wish to accomplish, use the eight R's to help you not just talk about it or dream about it but actually pull it off, my friend. You've got this!

Wow. That's a lot to cover in one book, but somehow we did it. Did you have a favorite chapter or a chapter that maybe wasn't your favorite because it challenged you the most? If so, please share your experience with me and the rest of the Shift Higher community online.

I sincerely say thank you! Thank you for giving me the chance to cultivate the potential inside you. Thank you for giving me the honor and opportunity to pour what I know and who I am into you through this book. Thank you for your commitment to yourself. Thank you for the action you're taking to better your best and live life to the fullest, because when you do that, you make this world a better place for all of us.

To help you with integrating all that you've learned, I offer you a list of a few of what I think are the best next steps.

Implementation Tips

- Keep this book on your desk, nightstand, bookshelf, or somewhere else close by. The more you see it, the more action you will take on its contents. Proximity is power.

- Share this book with your coworkers, colleagues, friends, family, and social groups. Encourage them to create a book club or discussion group around this book.

- Visit www.ShiftIntoAHigherGear.com for tons of free book bonuses and to join our amazing global online community of readers and implementers of this content.

- As I taught you in chapter 8, find an accountability partner and work together through your lessons, discoveries, goals, and action steps. Success is always better together.

- Take a selfie of yourself holding this book and tag me @Delatorro in it; encourage others to buy a copy of this book wherever books are sold.

- Give yourself a huge reward for finishing this book. Many people start, but you finished, my friend!

- Consider attending our Full Throttle Experience conference. Visit www.FullThrottleExperience.com/ShiftBook for a special message, invitation, and gift from me. I would love to meet you in person and facilitate a process where we can install these and other principles to help you shift into a higher gear in a fun, experiential, high-energy four-day live event.

Shift into a Higher Gear
Discussion Guide

Chapter 1

1. Shifts don't have to be big. What small changes can you make that will produce a difference, of any sort, in your life?

2. In order for you to better your best, you must top yourself in some small way on a regular basis. What three things can you change that will make you better in small ways every day?

3. Failure is not an option; it's a privilege reserved for those who try. How have you looked at "failure" in the past? How can you use it to build and grow? How can you focus more on your efforts and celebrate those as you achieve?

Chapter 2

1. When was the last time you celebrated a "Happy Width Day" and a "Happy Depth Day?" If you haven't, why not?

2. If you want to see all that life has to offer, you need to wear the right 3-D lenses. When was the last time you had a 3-D vision check that prompted you to live wide, long and deep?

3. Based on the number of summers you have left, my friend, what are you committed to doing, and who are you committed to being to live your life to the fullest?

Chapter 3

1. What or whom can you take to the next level right now simply by leaning more into it or into them with consistent action and enthusiasm?

2. What is the nail that you're lying on right now that hurts badly enough for you to complain, but not yet badly enough for you to change?

3. Is the change you seek a "should," an "ought to," or a "must"?

Chapter 4

1. Is there an area of your life that just needs more time? You're doing the right thing, but it just needs more time, more "wait" to manifest?

2. What is distracting you right now? What is that thinking that easily pulls you away from your goals and keeps you from being like a stamp and sticking to one thing until it delivers?

3. What are five "I am" statements that you will use to help you become the emotions you want to experience?

Chapter 5

1. We all have kickstands. What things in your life do you keep making excuses about, and why?

2. Cognitive reframing helps transform your life. What declarations can you repeat on a daily basis that will help you turn your problems into possibilities?

3. Fear has a way of using the facts of your life against you. This can hurt not only you but those around you. How can you do a better job focusing on truth instead of facts?

Chapter 6

1. Working harder on yourself is the catalyst for healthy relationships overall. In what ways can *you* build *you* in order to better serve others in your relationships?

2. What are three "fear into faith" declarations that you can implement now to transform and empower yourself to shift into a higher gear?

3. Fear doesn't want you to know that it's there, so it often disguises itself. What are three ways that fear tends to disguise itself in your life, career, and business, and how can you do a better job of recognizing it?

Chapter 7

1. Just like your physical home, your emotional home needs a lot of care. What are some self-care habits that you can implement to nourish your emotional home?

2. Before reading this book, had you ever considered what your *emotional address* was? Do you know what it is now and how it affects you and those around you whom you love and care about?

3. If you had the ability to become any five emotions you wanted to every single day, what would those emotions be?

Chapter 8

1. What did the posse audit reveal to you about the people who serve as a "plus" or a "minus" in your life? Are you pleased with your score? If not, what will you do to change it?

2. Do you have the right people riding with you in life? If not, what changes do you need to make so that you can arrive at your destination safely and enjoyably?

3. If you earned within $10K annually of your five closest coworkers, would you be pleased? If not, what do you need to do to better position yourself for promotion and career matriculation?

Chapter 9

1. Forgiveness is vital to forward movement. How can rolling the throttle on forgiveness help you get out of Park, Neutral, and Reverse?

2. What cycle are you tired of repeating in your life that bleeds over into other areas of your personal life?

3. Mediocrity can often show up in odd ways. Have you noticed areas where you have embraced it when you should have rejected it?

Chapter 10

1. Do you currently live your life as if the best has already happened? If so, what can you do to reposition yourself mental and emotionally to see the rest of your life as the best of your life?

2. We've all mastered the art of whining, complaining, and procrastinating. What can you do to move toward being a realist, an optimist, and an activist?

3. Do you function as the "King of the Jungle" in your role on a daily basis? If not, why? What limitations are you allowing to control your thoughts that you need to silence by focusing on your strengths?

Chapter 11

1. Did you know that rejection is actually valuable? In times past, how have you devalued rejection, and how can you look at it differently now?

2. Could you relate to the four potholes that Delatorro explained in the chapter? Are you avoiding them or running right over them without addressing the damage? What additional potholes have you encountered or could you encounter while on your journey?

3. In what ways have you ever experienced burnout? What do you do when this happens? How do you cope?

Chapter 12

1. Have you experienced goal setting, but not as much sustainable goal getting? What did the chapter's content on manifestation mean to you?

2. Are your goals written down in a place where you can see them? Do you have pictures or visuals to accompany them?

3. Which of the eight R's of accelerated goal achievement do you currently have in place? Which ones do you need to cultivate?

Notes

Introduction

1. Abbott, "What's the Secret to Living a Full Life? A New Global Survey Reveals Family Comes First," April 26, 2016, https://abbott.mediaroom.com/2016-04-26 -Whats-the-Secret-to-Living-a-Full-Life-A-New-Global-Survey-Reveals-Family -Comes-First.

Chapter 2

1. Max Roser, Esteban Ortiz-Ospina, and Hannah Ritchie, "Life Expectancy," Our World in Data, last revised October 2019, https://ourworldindata.org/life -expectancy#:~:text=The%20United%20Nations%20estimate%20a,life%20 expectancy%20of%2072.3%20years.

Chapter 5

1. Onder Hassan, "20 Excuses Most People Make That Stop Them from Reaching Their Dreams," Lifehack.org, January 25, 2021, https://www.lifehack.org/articles /communication/20-excuses-most-people-make-that-stop-them-from-reaching -their-dreams.html.

2. John Brandon, "10 Excuses Unproductive People Always Use," *Inc.*, July 10, 2014, https://www.inc.com/john-brandon/10-excuses-unproductive-people-always-use .html.

3. Linda Bloom, "Reframing," *Psychology Today*, December 14, 2017, https://www .psychologytoday.com/us/blog/stronger-the-broken-places/201712/reframing.

Chapter 6

1. Lisa Fritscher, "Could You Have Inherited Your Phobias?" Verywell Mind, October 23, 2020, https://www.verywellmind.com/research-findings-on-the-genetics-of -phobias-2671935.

2. Amy Morin, "Top 10 Fears That Hold People Back in Life," *Psychology Today*, January 28, 2020, https://www.psychologytoday.com/us/blog/what-mentally-strong -people-dont-do/202001/top-10-fears-hold-people-back-in-life.

3. John Fuhrman, *If They Say No, Just Say NEXT!* (Hummelstown, PA: Markowski International, 1999).

Chapter 7

1. Michael Miller, "7 Amazing Facts about Emotions You Should Know," Six Seconds, February 12, 2021, https://www.6seconds.org/2018/02/19/7-amazing-facts -emotions-know/.

Chapter 8

1. Quench USA, "Nearly 80 Percent of Working Americans Say They Don't Drink Enough Water: Quench Survey," *PR Newswire*, June 27, 2018, https://www.prnews wire.com/news-releases/nearly-80-percent-of-working-americans-say-they-dont -drink-enough-water-quench-survey-300668537.html.

2. Sarah Kathleen Peck, "Why Your Most Important Business Move Might Be Joining a Mastermind," *Forbes*, July 17, 2018, https://www.forbes.com/sites/sarahkathleen peck/2018/02/21/why-you-should-join-a-mastermind/?sh=56ce9d7d3197.

Chapter 10

1. Mark Beech, "Disney's 'Lion King' Tops $11.6 Billion on Anniversary, Most Successful Franchise Ever," *Forbes*, October 30, 2019, https://www.forbes.com/sites /markbeech/2019/10/30/lion-king-tops-116-billion-on-anniversary-most -successful-franchise-ever/?sh=2df40b8f1c0a.

Chapter 11

1. Mason Stevenson, "Employee Burnout Statistics You Need to Know," HR Exchange Network, January 16, 2020, https://www.hrexchangenetwork.com /employee-engagement/news/employee-burnout-statistics-you-need-to-know.

2. Ibid.

3. "Study Sees Rise in Lonely Americans, and the Workplace Might Play a Part," *Occupational Health & Safety*, January 28, 2020, https://ohsonline.com/Articles

/2020/01/28/Study-Sees-Rise-in-Lonely-Americans-and-the-Workplace-Might -Play-a-Part.aspx?Page=1 OH&S Online.

4. "Mental Health Statistics: Stress," Mental Health Foundation, January 16, 2020, https://www.mentalhealth.org.uk/statistics/mental-health-statistics-stress.

5. Rachel Gillett, "How Walt Disney, Oprah Winfrey, and 19 Other Successful People Rebounded after Getting Fired," *Inc.*, https://www.inc.com/business-insider/21 -successful-people-who-rebounded-after-getting-fired.html.

6. "How Many Times Was Chicken Soup for the Soul Rejected?" Feeling Success, December 17, 2015, http://feelingsuccess.com/?p=5857.

7. Alison Millington, "J.K. Rowling's Pitch for 'Harry Potter' Was Rejected 12 Times," *Insider*, July 30, 2018, https://www.insider.com/revealed-jk-rowlings-original-pitch -for-harry-potter-2017-10.

8. Jay Mathews, "The Education of Steven Spielberg. It Didn't Involve Ivy." *Washington Post*, July 10, 2019, https://www.washingtonpost.com/local/education/the -education-of-steven-spielberg-it-didnt-involve-ivy/2019/07/09/9add0470-a262 -11e9-b732-41a79c2551bf_story.html.

9. Riz Pasha, "Walt Disney Was Fired & Rejected 300 Times," SucceedFeed, January 26, 2018, https://succeedfeed.com/walt-disney-was-fired-rejected-300-times.

10. "Vincent van Gogh Biography," Van Gogh Gallery, https://www.vangoghgallery .com/misc/biography.html.

Index

About the Author

For nearly two decades, the name **Delatorro McNeal, II** has been synonymous with high achievement, excellence, infectious energy, and transformational content. As a best-selling author, global keynote speaker, and peak performance expert, Delatorro has set the stage and created platforms for people from all walks of life. His work ethic, experience, wisdom, testimony, and ability to create life analogies make him one of the most respected experts in the personal development industry.

Del has spoken in forty-nine of the fifty US states and abroad, delivering more than four thousand presentations over the past twenty years. He has presented to major corporations, professional associations, annual conventions, pro sports teams, churches, and leadership conferences. Notable clients include Johnson & Johnson, New York Life, JP Morgan Chase, Prudential, and the Million Dollar Round Table.

Delatorro earned a master's degree in instructional systems design with an emphasis in human performance enhancement from the Florida State University. His personal mission is to help individuals and organizations grow to the next level. As the author of eight books and over a dozen personal growth and professional development courses, online courses, and coaching programs, he has utilized his education to pull others into a place of peak performance in all aspects of their lives.

Delatorro holds the prestigious CSP (Certified Speaking Professional) designation, which is the highest international recognition of professional speaking excellence, and he is in the top 12% of paid professional speakers worldwide. He has been featured on national and international television networks, including Fox, ABC, NBC, BET, TBN, Daystar, and Oxygen. His voice and works have also been heard on syndicated radio shows across America.

Delatorro is the founder of the Full Throttle Experience, a four-day annual experiential personal development conference hosted in Florida. Enthralled by this highly energetic, motorcycle-themed leadership and business success event, crowds are left in amazement and catapulted to greater dimensions.

As a peak performance expert, Delatorro partners with Fortune 500 corporations, professional associations, and entrepreneurs to drastically improve their organizational effectiveness, employee morale, and productivity. He also provides training and development courses that mature teamwork, sales performance, and communication strategies.

Delatorro travels the globe, empowering diverse audiences with his hard-hitting, experiential, high-energy, content-rich, and paradigm-shifting keynotes, seminars, and extreme team-building programs. He is a proud and active member of the National Speakers Association and the Global Speakers Federation.

When Delatorro is not traveling the world or dropping wisdom in virtual and in-person events, he is known in his greatest role as a father to his girls, Miracle and Hope.

Empowering You to Grow to the Next Level

I love being a lifelong learner. It's a core part of who I am. Every high achiever I know is also a lifelong learner, because one thing we all know and understand is that the learning never stops. Growth is perpetual.

So we've made it super easy for you to continue to grow with us.

As a reader of this book, you are entitled to free bonuses! Yay! ☺

You can find a free bonus chapter, great bonus videos, and extra supporting content centered around this book by visiting **ShiftIntoAHigher Gear.com** today.

Would you allow me to be a virtual mentor to you? I took my thirty favorite concepts from this book and created a powerful online course called Shift with Delatorro. In this online course, which includes more than thirty powerful videos, downloadable PDF worksheets, and course tracking for accountability, I reinforce many of the principles from this book to help you grow and develop at a more accelerated rate. Visit **ShiftWithDelatorro .com** to enroll today.

Do you represent an organization and you're looking for a dynamic speaker for your next event? If so, visit **Delatorro.com** to learn how I can serve as a keynote speaker, presentation skills trainer, or NLP practitioner for your upcoming event.

Are you ready to shift your sales into a higher gear? If so, allow me to teach you one of the most important skills you'll ever learn in business:

the art of persuasive presentation. We have a powerful online course called Crush Your Sales, and its sole purpose is to teach you exactly how to set up, deliver, and convert your clients and customers using persuasive presentation skills. Visit **CrushTheSale.com** to learn more and enroll.

Do you enjoy listening to podcasts that inspire, motivate, and challenge you to be your best? Then check out our "Crushing Life with Delatorro" podcast. Find it on your favorite podcasting platform. I teach you how to develop the mindset, heartset, skillset, and willset to lead and live an extraordinary quality of life right now. Do you have the desire to speak onstage and develop your public speaking skills with me as your coach and mentor? Would you like to work with me directly . . . live? Learn my coveted twelve-step blueprint for presentation skills mastery so you can speak with confidence, win your audience, and grow your bank account. Visit **HelpMeCrushTheStage.com** to learn the dates for our next training cohort and enroll today.

Remember, the biggest room in the world is room for improvement!

Shift into a higher gear with me in any of these amazing ways!

Do you love listening to inspiring, empowering content through Podcasts?

WELCOME TO THE

CRUSHING LIFE *with* *Delatorro* ★ PODCAST

The goal of our show is to help you develop the Mindset, Heartset, Skillset and Willset to live and lead an extraordinary quality of life right now!

Find us on your favorite podcasting platform.

www.CrushingLifePodcast.com

If you really want to Shift Your Job/Career/
Business into a Higher Gear, you must learn how to sell!
With over 2 decades of experience in persuasive presentation

DR. DELATORRO'S ONLINE
COURSE CALLED

CRU$H
Y O U R
ALE

is the ideal platform that will teach you how to Package,
Position and Pitch your products and services with
excellence to your clients, prospects
and customers.

Visit **www.CrushTheSale.com** to learn more and enroll today!

Dear reader,

Thank you for picking up this book and welcome to the worldwide BK community! You're joining a special group of people who have come together to create positive change in their lives, organizations, and communities.

What's BK all about?

Our mission is to connect people and ideas to create a world that works for all.

Why? Our communities, organizations, and lives get bogged down by old paradigms of self-interest, exclusion, hierarchy, and privilege. But we believe that can change. That's why we seek the leading experts on these challenges—and share their actionable ideas with you.

A welcome gift

To help you get started, we'd like to offer you a **free copy** of one of our bestselling ebooks:

www.bkconnection.com/welcome

When you claim your **free ebook**, you'll also be subscribed to our blog.

Our freshest insights

Access the best new tools and ideas for leaders at all levels on our blog at ideas.bkconnection.com.

Sincerely,

Your friends at Berrett-Koehler